The Tagus and the Tiber; or, Notes of travel in Portugal, Spain, and Italy, in 1850-1.

William Edward Baxter

смет с. 18.

THE TAGUS

AND THE TIBER.

VOL. II.

LONDON :
R. CLAY, PRINTER, BREAD STREET HILL.

THE TAGUS

AND THE TIBER;

OR,

NOTES OF TRAVEL IN PORTUGAL,

SPAIN, AND ITALY,

IN 1850-1.

BY

WILLIAM EDWARD BAXTER.

IN TWO VOLUMES.

VOL. II.

LONDON:

RICHARD BENTLEY, NEW BURLINGTON STREET,

Publisher in Ordinary to Her Majesty.

1852.

CONTENTS OF THE SECOND VOLUME.

CHAPTER I.

CHAPTER II.

CHAPTER III.

CHAPTER IV.

NOTES ON THE RUINS OF ROME.

CHAPTER VII.

NOTES ON THE POLITICAL CONDITION OF ITALY.

CHAPTER VIII.

NOTES ON THE POLITICAL INFLUENCE OF ROMAN CATHOLICISM.

CHAPTER IX.

NOTES ON THE POLITICAL INFLUENCE OF ROMAN CATHOLICISM,
continued.

CHAPTER X.

NOTES ON THE LAND QUESTION AT HOME AND ABROAD.

CHAPTER XI.

NOTES ON THE EDUCATION OF THE PEOPLE AT HOME AND ABROAD.

THE TAGUS
AND THE TIBER.

CHAPTER I.

IN a former work I have recorded my impressions
of Milan, the scene of the Viscontis' cruelties,
the city of Ambrose, the stern disciplinarian of

kings, and of Angilbertus, who in the ninth century maintained a steady opposition to the corruptions of Rome.* We had stopped on this occasion in our journey towards the south, merely to spend a day or two in admiring that unrivalled cathedral, which Willis, in his Pencillings by the Way, characterises as " too delicate and beautiful for the open air." When we entered the spacious aisles on the morning of the succeeding day, the Archbishop had just concluded the ceremony of baptizing three children, the performance of which annually some time-sanctioned custom has enjoined. But the roof of the Duomo is the place to enjoy the elaborate carving, the thousand statues, the graceful minarets, the light buttresses and massive slabs—all of pure white marble—which render this edifice so deservedly celebrated among the Churches of Europe. To Napoleon we are indebted for much that now delights the eye; for although begun in 1386, the building progressed but slowly until he applied to its advancement the resources of his unconquerable will. Even now many spires and statues are wanting to complete

* See " Milner's Church History," Century IX. chap. iii.

the original design; but the edifice does not look unfinished, for each minaret has a figure on its summit, and statues, the work of famous artists, fill the niches in these aërial towers.

· In the centre a lofty pyramid supports a gilt representation of the Virgin, around which cluster pinnacles of exquisite proportions, like a miniature city of spires. None of the great European Churches to my mind at all equal, in point of exterior elegance, the Cathedral of Milan. When the evening sun shines on its fairy-like architecture, it appears like the temple of the Celestial City, fashioned by angelic intelligences; or, to use the words of Mrs. Hemans,—

> "A mountain of white marble, steep'd ·
> In light, like floating gold."

In clear weather the traveller may enjoy from the top a view of no common splendour, comprising the city, with its churches, convents, barracks, arches, and palaces, the rich plain of Lombardy, the Apennines, and every peak of the higher Alps, from the snow-white Orteles in the Tyrol, to Mont Blanc, Monta Rosa rising at no great distance from your point of observation—the monarch of the scene. The oftener I returned to gaze on this wonderful creation, the more my mind was filled with admiration, both of its design and of its execution. Elaborate ornament seldom indeed succeeds in producing an effect so majestic and sublime. Again and again I sauntered round it, and finally went away quite convinced that no such temple has yet been erected for the worship of God.

The sights of Milan I had seen previously; our only other visit, therefore, was to the old Church of St. Ambrose, said to be the same into which that intrepid man refused to admit the Emperor Theodosius. With all his faults of temper, it has ever appeared to me that Ambrose was a great and good man. He lived in an age when religious toleration was unknown, when men oftentimes mistook their own impulses for heavenly light; but although stern, he was " in labours abundant;" though superstitious, he fervently sought guidance from on high; though unmerciful to Arians, he devoted his estate to the poor. While alive he manfully struggled for " the faith once delivered to the saints," in opposition to the dignities of the empire; and he died esteemed and regretted by every well-wisher of that Church, which heresy threatened to destroy.

In the year 1844, the Corso, or Boulevard which surrounds the city of Milan, presented on fine summer evenings an animated spectacle of carriages and equestrians, rich liveries, and gaily-dressed fashionables: it was pleasant then to sit under the elms, and look, on the one hand, towards the Alpine summits tinged by the setting sun; on the other, at the glittering pageant which these pleasure-seekers displayed. Now all is changed. On the evening of a festival, I sauntered along this spacious drive, and found it forsaken, desolate, lonely. Here and there a grim Austrian soldier guarded a cannon, or a tradesman and his wife jogged along in a rickety gig; but the nobles, the equipages, the prancing steeds, had all disappeared,—gone to Turin, to Paris, to London,— to any place where the hated uniforms of Hapsburg are not seen. Those who remain have sold their studs, appear seldom in public, and, living retired and obscure, wait the good time coming, when

Hungary shall sound the loud tocsin, and Austria, paralysed, behold the political emancipation of Italy.

I had observed, during my previous visit to Lombardy, the dislike felt by all classes towards their German masters. No one even then could spend a few days in Verona, Padua, and especially Venice, without observing it; but that dislike was love, in comparison with the unconcealed hatred, the ungovernable detestation, expressed in 1851, by man, woman, and child, when speaking of "i Tedeschi." We travelled always in the public conveyances, and conversed with a great many people in every walk of life; but we only met one man (and he was a Tuscan officer) who did not openly avow himself an advocate of national independence, a sworn enemy of the bayonets of the north. In Bologna, in Florence, in Rome, in Leghorn, in Pisa, but most of all in Milan, did this dislike manifest itself. In none of these cities, nor on any of the roads in the country, did we see a single German officer or soldier speaking to an Italian. The military rulers have been everywhere sent to Coventry; and when new commotions take place across the Alps, they will be sent somewhere else with very little ceremony.

I looked for any mark of intercourse between the people and the troops in the streets, in the churches, in the carriages, and at the balconies of the capital of Lombardy, but in vain. There are two principal cafés, occupying different sides of the Piazzo del Duomo. The Café Mazza was always full of Austrian officers, not a single Italian ever entering it; while the Milanese gentlemen and ladies crowded the café opposite; and if a German dared to intrude there, every citizen instantly rose and departed. Tobacco is, as many know, a Government monopoly. To injure the revenue of their detested rulers, the Lombards have given up using it; not a man was to be seen smoking in the streets; and scarcely had I entered that, as well as other cities, when I was warned not to put a cigar into my mouth, and thereby break the rules of the "Invisible Government." "If you smoke, Sir, you will be knocked down," was repeatedly re-marked to me; and who would not respect the feelings of a people, kept in check by the armed soldiery of a power which Kossuth has well called the mere "satellite" of Russia, yet scorning to associate in any degree with their oppressors? One of the national poets has mournfully exclaimed,—

"Italia! in te acetata e disunita;"

but although, to enslave that unfortunate country, the despots of the north have combined, and her sons, torn by intestine quarrels, not true to themselves, have as yet been unsuccessful in counteracting their oppressors' plots, let us not forget that wise saying of Ovid's,—

"Neque enim lex æquior ulla
Quam necis artifices arte perire sua."

How much more polite than their transalpine neighbours are the people of sunny Italy! We had scarcely spent one day in Milan before this fact forced itself upon our observation. In the streets, in public places, everywhere room was made for us; and no one jostled our elbows, stared rudely at us, or puffed tobacco into our eyes.

Sunday was the feast of Pentecost. We went to the cathedral just in time to see the curtain of the grand door drawn up, and the archbishop, a fine-looking man, enter, superbly dressed, with a mitre glittering with jewels, and attended by priests, nuns, and footmen in splendid liveries. A dense crowd assembled at mass; and after the reading of the gospel, the prelate himself preached in Italian, which he does only three times a-year. He read his discourse out of a book : I was not near enough to see whether in manuscript or printed; but my next neighbour remarked that he could do that himself, if that were all the ability required in a minister. I was somewhat surprised to observe so many men at the confessionals,— a very unusual sight in the present age.

We left Milan on Monday, the ninth of June, in the *intérieur* of the diligence for Bologna; and, driving out of the southern gate, had a fine view beyond the green mulberry-trees of the far distant Orteles in the Tyrol, its dome of spotless snow rising above the plain of Lombardy, the delicious valley which Shakspeare calls "the pleasant garden of great Italy." In the forty-second chapter of Gibbon's "Decline and Fall of the Roman Empire," there occurs a striking passage regarding the origin and manners of that strange people who, from the banks of the Elbe and the Oder, crossed the Alps, and finally settled on the Po. Whoever wishes to know the history of a nation now trodden under foot, must read this graphic account; and perhaps, on rising from its perusal, a thought may cross his mind that the descendants of those Langobards whom Alboin led to the very gates of Ravenna, may yet, if the signal be given, re-enact the fearful scenes which took place on the Danube when the Gepidæ were destroyed.

Travellers in Central Australia tell us of heat so excessive that the leaves fell off the trees, and the mercury burst the bulb of the thermometer. How they survived withering blasts which silenced birds, prostrated horses, and ignited matches,* must remain for ever a mystery to me, for the power of the sun which shone upon us during our journey to Bologna seemed enough to paralyse any ordinary man. The leaves hung motionless on the trees, a quivering heat trembled among the ears of corn, and clouds of dust shrouded our vehicle.

* See Captain Sturt's "Expedition into Central Australia."

Melegnano is pleasantly situated on the river Lambro, in the midst of a country remarkable for its fertility, irrigated on the most scientific principles by means of canals, watercourses, sluices, and aqueducts, and producing great quantities of grain. Formerly this part of Lombardy was a forest, but the Muzza canal, with its various branches, has transformed it into a garden, whose agricultural resources excite the envy of less favoured provinces. I observed very fine fields of maize, clover, rye, and other plants, separated from each other by somewhat tiresome rows of melancholy willow-trees. The rice-plantations were all under water.

The second place at which we stopped—Lodi—recals the memories of other days; for that bridge over the Adda two gallant armies struggled in terrific combat, and there Napoleon's soldiers rushed on the artillerymen of Austria, shouting *Vive la République!* In the district around this place is made the famous Parmesan cheese, so called because it was first exported from Parma. They likewise cultivate flax to a considerable extent. Beyond Castarepusterlengo, where hundreds of people in holiday costume had assembled to celebrate a festival, we passed a great number of clover-fields, covered with water from the canals, in default of rain.

We now came in sight of the peaks of the Apennines, and after journeying for a mile or two on the top of the embankment raised to protect the country from the inundations of the Po, stopped for an unreasonably long time at the frontier of Lombardy to have our passports *viséed*.   Between Milan and Bologna I had to show that document no fewer than fourteen times to the authorities, and to submit to three custom-house examinations of luggage.   Several people had been stopped on account of trivial informalities; and one Sardinian gentleman, in whose company I afterwards crossed the Apennines, informed me that the authorities at Castelfranco, a miserable village on the frontier of the States of the Church, detained him there for three days, because the signature of one Papal delegate instead of another was attached to his passport.   So much for the freedom of travelling in this part of Italy!

We crossed the broad and rapid Po by a temporary and somewhat insecure bridge of boats, leading to the ancient town of Piacenza, which occupies an imposing situation on the right bank of the river. Its principal square is considered, justly I think, one of the finest in the peninsula. As if determined to incur the ridicule of every rational being, the government of this petty state, a mere second-rate satellite of Austria, are at present engaged in throwing away money on new fortifications. A Parisian who travelled with us in the diligence, with propriety remarked, that it seemed to him a return to barbarism.

An uninteresting road, the same formerly called the Via Emilia, having been made by Emilius Lepidus in the sixth century, conducts from Piacenza to Parma, the capital of the duchy, which was a city of some note long before the Christian era, but has now a gloomy, deserted look, many of the large mansions being untenanted.

At the frontier of the duchy of Modena we were detained fifty minutes, whilst the "active" officials examined two trunks and sealed five boxes of merchandise; and at Reggio, a flourishing town, chiefly remarkable as the birthplace of Correggio and Ariosto, the diligence remained an hour with-

out any reason at all. On leaving it we passed
through a pretty country, and crossed the dry beds
of several mountain-torrents, the channels which
carry off the melted snows of the neighbouring
Apennines, whose white peaks we saw towering
above the mulberry-trees. The vines, hung in
festoons from tree to tree, add materially to the
beauty of the landscape; but the houses are poor,
dirty, and uncomfortable, and the district swarms
with beggars. We stopped for some time at Modena, capital of the duchy of the same name, a
curious old place of thirty thousand inhabitants,
which has long been governed by the Este family,
and where they have a library of ten thousand
volumes. Its lofty cathedral-spire rises very conspicuously in the flat plain.

For several miles after passing the Pope's frontier, we had an escort of dragoons, this part of
Italy being, perhaps, the most robber-infested
district in Europe. Some weeks afterwards I observed in the *Journal des Debats* that the diligence
had been attacked here by banditti, who murdered
several soldiers before taking to flight. In the
Legations especially, one cannot travel with any

degree of security; for the people hate their rulers, both Papal and Austrian, who, unassisted by the peasantry, have been utterly unable to exterminate the predatory bands whose outrages every now and then fill Italy with dread.

A writer in the Quarterly Review has attempted to turn into ridicule the statement which I made in a former volume, that Lombardy was beautifully cultivated, while its peasanty live in hovels, and are clothed in rags. Great is the astonishment affected by this critic that a country could look like a garden, and at the same time its population be miserable. Apparently profoundly ignorant of the system of middlemen and absenteeism, of rack-renting and extortion, by which the real cultivators of the soil in the valley of the Po have been reduced to the level of the lower classes in Tipperary, my Mentor treats the remarks which appear to him contradictory, as the result of visual obliquity, and dismisses them with a compassionating smile.

The ancient and well-known city of Bologna stands in a plain carpeted with the beautiful hemp plant, at the base of the first spur of the Apennines.

Its narrow streets, archways, piazzas, and spires, recal to one's mind the days of Italy's republics, when civil warfare desolated the peninsula. The tower of Asinelli, three hundred and twenty-seven feet high, becomes visible long before you see the houses of the town. Within a few feet of it stands a mis-shaped tower, built in 1100, one hundred and forty-five feet in height, which leans eight feet out of the perpendicular. The two together have a strange appearance.

In the chief square is the ugly church dedicated to St. Petronius, where Charles V. was crowned by Clement VII. Hallam tells us that "if it were necessary to construe the word *university* in the strict sense of a legal incorporation, Bologna might lay claim to a higher antiquity than either Paris or Oxford." *

As a school of Roman jurisprudence it acquired great celebrity, and Tiraboschi says that in the beginning of the thirteenth century there were ten thousand young men there pursuing their studies. In the year 1580, according to the state papers relating to the province, and addressed to the

* History of the Middle Ages, vol. ii. p. 481.

Legate, " Fa da 130m. anime la città 70m. che avanti le carestie 90m. Ha 400 fra carozze e cocchi. Vengono nella città ogni anno da 600m. libre de follicelli da quali si fa la seta, e se ne mette opera per uso della città 100m. libre l'anno." Like other cities in the Papal States, it has rather declined than increased in prosperity, and now when travellers cross the Alps, and Pyrenees, and Carpathians with perfect safety, banditti prowl on every road near Bologna.

It was yet only four o'clock in the morning, when, seated in the interior of the diligence, we left this city for Florence. For two hours our route lay up a cheerful valley, the ground being very uneven. Then commenced a steep ascent, which lasted, with some intermissions, for six hours, and several times oxen assisted our horses to drag the vehicle. Here, too, the vines hung in beautiful festoons from the branches.

As we mounted higher and higher on the Apennines, a most extensive prospect revealed itself of the plain of Lombardy, with the deep ravines, great limestone cliffs, bold peaks, green hill-sides, and stony valleys of the mountains which we

traversed.   The excellent road, without rut or
stone, wound round their unequal and fantastically-
shaped shoulders, and at every steep ascent old
women, mothers with children, boys, and girls ran
after us to beg. " Buona signora, una cosa, una
cosina," rang for hours in our ears.   These heights
are frequently exposed, even in summer, to violent
gales; it in fact blew hard when we crossed them.
The picturesque situations occupied by the villages
reminded me more than once of Mr. Macaulay's
animated lines, in which he alludes to them as—

> " Eagle's nests
> Perch'd on the crests
> Of purple Apennine."

At the poor hamlet of La Cas we passed the Pope's
frontier, and soon afterwards stopped at Filigari,
where our passports were *viséed* and our luggage
examined by the officers of the Duke of Tuscany.
In the miserable inn two small lean chickens and
vermicelli water, professing to be soup, were presented to seven hungry travellers as their mid-day
meal; while the " vino bianco " and the " vino
rosso " were equally undrinkable.   Chestnut-trees
grow in great abundance on the hills around these

villages; but dreary mountains, reminding me strongly of Spain, had to be crossed after leaving them. Heavy falls of snow frequently render this part of the road impassable in winter.

Descending from these desolate heights into a valley with well-tilled fields, and, what are very unusual abroad, a few country seats, we followed the banks of a little stream, up a narrow highland glen to Fontebuona, the last changing-place, where I got out of the diligence and walked up a steep hill, from the top of which a view burst upon my senses, which language fails to describe. It was a cloudless warm evening, the sun shining brilliantly, and a pleasant breeze playing among the foliage of the gardens around; there lay the Val d'Arno, with its woods and winding stream; while, as it were beneath my feet, glittering in Italian sunshine, rose the domes and towers of Florence; on the left, crowning a lofty hill, was Virgil's Fiesole, and far as the eye could reach white houses sparkled like jewels on the purple Apennines. A delicious fragrance from the vine-yards filled the air,—peasants returning to their homes dashed past me in their light vehicles,

and music, rising and falling with the gentle wind,
broke upon my ear. Lost in admiration, I sat
down on a bank, where the wild thyme grew, and
meditated on the scene before me.

"Talia Fesuleo lentus meditabar in antro
Rure sub urbano Medicum, qua mons sacer urbem
Mæoniam, longique volumina despicit Arni." *

As we approached nearer " the fair white walls
of the Etrurian Athens," the view became, if possible, more striking; but at length we reached
the arch of Francis I., and entered the city, the
first men we saw within the gates being Austrian
soldiers, a race whom the Florentines hold in utter
aversion. As in Milan and Bologna, we observed
that no communication of any kind passed between
the citizens and the military; they dwell together
in anything but amity, and take little pains to
conceal their mutual antipathy. " Non durerà,"

* The reader will, perhaps, remember the opening of chapter
ii. in the sixth book of that splendid historical romance, "Rienzi,
the Last of the Tribunes :"—" It was a bright, oppressive, sultry
morning, when a solitary horseman was seen winding that un-
equalled road from whose height, amidst fig-trees, vines, and
olives, the traveller beholds gradually break upon his gaze the
enchanting valley of the Arno and the spires and domes of
Florence."

exclaimed an Italian to me, with a vehemence quite startling, "perchè, perchè signor, abbiamo in cielo un Dio giusto."

Few educated Englishmen require to be told the situation of Florence, "girt by her theatre of hills" and divided into two portions by the silvery Arno. Its walls, seven miles in circumference, enclose a population of about one hundred thousand; and in its narrow and bustling, but admirably paved streets, the noble mansions of the ancient nobility, with their extensive gardens, may be seen side by side with dwellings of the meanest kind. The massive blocks of hewn stone, each standing out into relief in its separate grandeur, and all combining to form palaces fit for royalty, tell of former days, when the Bardi and the Peruzzi farmed the customs of England and Sicily, and the Medici brought both merchandise and manuscripts from the furthest regions of the East; when Cosmo devoted his wealth to the restoration of learning, and Lorenzo sat between Raffaelle d'Urbino and Michael Angelo Buonarotti in the Platonic academy.*

* See Vasari's " Vite dei Pittori."

To the little Florentine republic the literature and arts of Europe owe more than to all those powerful nations combined, which by turns over-ran Tuscany with their armies. There Dante Alighieri, the Milton of Italy, the parent of its poetry, first saw the light, and there one hundred years afterwards Boccaccio, at the command of the civic rulers, read lectures on the Divine Comedy, not excepting that famous philippic against an ungrateful country in the sixteenth canto del Paradiso, beginning " O poca nostra nobiltà di sangue." A citizen too of this Athens, retiring on account of political differences to Arezzo, became the father of Petrarch, the poet of love and friendship, of religion and glory, whose Laura has been celebrated with all the music of his native tongue. And then Florence was the home of the improvisatori, the extempore verse-makers, who, from village to village, at every festa and rural dance, expressed, in recitative eclogues, the charms of Italian beauty. Nor can we forget the revolutions, the alarms, the massacres, the proscriptions, the political changes which took place during even the palmy days of Tuscan greatness, the quarrels between the nobles and the populace, or that enactment, unique of its kind, by which the latter, then triumphant, excepted, from the edict banishing the higher classes, five hundred persons, whom they declared RAISED from being patricians to the ranks of the commoners.

Even in pure democracies at the present time, wealth or official·rank creates a sort of nobility; but the great families of Florence strove for the *privilege* of being esteemed plebeian; proud and domineering when " la ruota di fortuna " revolved in their favour, many of them in adverse circumstances swam with the tide, while others retired to their strongholds on the crests of the Apennines, watching, like keen-eyed vultures, their time to pounce on the prey. Driven from their palaces on account of their licence and tyranny, these *Fuorusciti* plotted, now with the Guelfs, then with the Ghibellines, to subvert the dominant faction and restore themselves to power.*

* " Vecchia fama nel mondo li chiama orbi,
　　Gente avara, invidiosa, e superba
　　Da' lor costumi fa che tu ti forbi."
Dante's " Inferno," canto 15.

CHAPTER II.

ONE cannot spend half a day in Florence without
observing, with surprise, the numerous evidences
of English residence. Such sign-boards as the
following indicate the degree to which the inhabitants are indebted to foreign capital:—" Joseph
Gamgeau, veterinary surgeon." " George Graff,
coachmaker in all its branches." " Excellent
riding horses on hire." " Rafael Betti Cook sends

out dinners." "James Huband's livery stables." "English apothecary." "Thomas Price's Olympic Circus." "Furnishing shop." "Rose & Co., Tailors." "Abernethy biscuits sold here." "Goodban, printseller." You meet fellow-countrymen in every street; and many of the carriages which drive past appear to have been importations from London. A stranger would feel a difficulty in deciding whether "Inglesi" or friars most abound in the Tuscan metropolis: he sees both everywhere,—the latter as dirty and disagreeable looking as the former are clean and of pleasing countenance. The citizens have a curious custom of wheeling about prints and other cotton goods in barrows for sale, instead of erecting attractive shops to allure customers. Their manners struck me as deferential and friendly; without grimace or theatrical compliments, they treat visitors with a politeness exceedingly gratifying.

The name of the Pitti Palace, now the residence of the Grand Duke, is quite familiar to northern ears. Those who have studied the actions of Lorenzo de Medici, will recollect that this mag-

nificent edifice was planned by the conspirator
Luca Pitti, and that when his intrigues met with
their merited punishment, the progress of the
works was stopped; but not until as much had
been built as immortalized the name of the envious
noble. Speaking of the various erections ordered
by this Florentine, Macchiavelli says, — " Ma
quello nella Citta al tutto maggiore che alcon altro
che da privato cittadino fino à quel giorno fusse
stato edificato." It stands on an elevation on the
left bank of the Arno, and is connected with the
ancient ducal palace, in the principal square of the
city, by a covered bridge, which crosses both the
houses and the river. The Boboli gardens rise
immediately behind it, occupying the slope and
summit of a gentle eminence. The view from the
tower on the highest point, though not so extensive
as that from the neighbouring mountains, perhaps
exceeds it in mellowed beauty. Emerging from
avenues of noble trees and groves of lemons, which
fountains cool and statues adorn, you suddenly
behold stretched out, as in a panorama, the domes
and palaces, the hanging gardens and villas em-

bosomed in wood, which justify Rogers in exclaiming,—

"Of all the cities on the earth,
There's none so fair as Florence."

But returning to the main entrance, let us ascend to the second story, and visit those fifteen saloons, where the traveller, in the glowing words of Byron, becomes " dazzled and drunk with beauty." Frescoes by celebrated masters adorn the ceilings of these apartments; and on their walls hang the treasures of art which, if they charm the eye, mock the descriptive powers of every author. The collections at Munich, Dresden, and Madrid, may be much more extensive; but the Pitti Palace contains few, if any works by second-rate artists: it is a mine of the purest gold, and baser metal has been excluded. In the same space, a like exhibition of masterpieces nowhere exists. There you find that famous portrait of Leo X., by Rafael, before which Cardinal Pescia knelt and presented bulls for signature. Three centuries have passed away since this painting was executed, yet even now I could imagine a similar mistake to be committed; for the vigorous colouring, the proud

attitude, the bold relief in which the figure stands
out, even the minute details of dress and ornament,
conspire to cause an illusion almost irresistible
Then you have Guido's Bacchus, and Murillo's
Madonna; but it were folly to enumerate. I only
mention two more, chiefly because they appeared
to me unspeakably superior to all the others, and
because whilst I write, copies of them, very cleverly
executed by my friend, Signor Petrini of Florence,
hang before me.

To those who can appreciate the inexpressible
charm possessed by Guido's pictures, it is no small
praise to say that some connoisseurs consider the
grandest of all his works to be " The Cleopatra "
in this collection. With a countenance turned towards heaven, and expressive of a deep yet controlled agony, she applies the asp to her bosom;
while on a table beside her is the basket of figs, in
which the reptile had been conveyed. In her face
you read the memorable history of Egypt's enchanting queen. Sick of a world whose changes
vex her, wearied of a life devoted to degrading
sin, doubtful of the future whither her spirit must
soon take its flight, she casts her glassy eyes

upwards to the seat of Deity, and communicates the poison to her veins. Stranger, behold her look of anguish, the awful emotions of that perturbed spirit, on which the world has in vain lavished its pleasures, and know what it is to be " chained to the chariot of triumphal Art."

Close to one of those sensual, vulgar groups, which Peter Paul Rubens calls Holy Families, hangs the most celebrated of the Virgins of Raffaelle, the lovely Madonna della Segiola, repetitions of which abound in every country under the sun. Mary, seated on a couch, tenderly embraces the infant Jesus, and leans her head so as almost to touch His noble brow; while the young St. John, with his hands in the attitude of adoration, worships the Babe whose name is Wonderful. What a heavenly group! It speaks of a better world, where saints repose with confidence in the bosom of their Lord. A tender mother, yet a humble believer, happy but serious, the Virgin folds in her arms the Child in whose countenance one can read Divinity. There is no familiarity, no unlikely prostration; you see a pious parent musing on the mysterious ways of Providence, while the glance of the Infant's eye seems to penetrate the heart of the observer, and to whisper, in angelic accents, "I am He." The softness of touch, the ease of attitude, the gracefulness of conception, the natural colouring, all attest this splendid picture to be the work of him who "pingere posse animam atque oculis præbere videndum;" *par excellence*, the painter of expression, the delineator of the soul.

In Raffaelle's masterpieces, art exists in its highest possible manifestations, without being seen; everything is regular, yet not constrained; and richness never degenerates into pomposity. He frequently, by a series of happy touches, represents the progress of a scene and the rapidly-changing emotions of the actors. Vasari narrates that a Bolognese artist, who had long wished to see a work by the great master, on opening the case which contained one, was so overpowered with conflicting feelings, that he sickened and died. Where movement and passion had to be represented, no one could equal him. The Virgin, to whom he especially devoted his powers, appears in some of his works the simple Mary of Bethlehem, the guileless peasant of Judea; in others, the majestic queen of angels, enthroned in clouds, and attended by the seraphs who proclaimed her Son. So famous did he become in Rome, "ut quasi cœleste demissum numen, ad æternam urbem in pristinam majestatem reparandam, omnes homines suspiciant."

In the centre of a small anteroom stands the celebrated Venus by Canova. Perhaps some people may consider it exceedingly bad taste, on my part, to say that this statue disappointed me more than any other work of art in Italy; yet I cannot help remarking, that the visitors to the American department of the Great Exhibition have seen, in my opinion, a far nobler piece of sculpture, viz. Hiram Power's Greek Slave. Mr. Ruskin remarks, in his "Stones of Venice,"— "The admiration of Canova I hold to be one of the deadliest symptoms of the civilization of the upper classes in the present century." This statement requires to be qualified and explained, for some of the tombs executed by that artist have obtained for him a position from which he cannot be dislodged by a mere sentence; but certainly the raptures affected by some people on beholding

the Venus must remain to me incomprehensible.
It possesses no distinctive feature enabling you at
once to characterise it as the queen of love and
beauty, the mother of Cupid and mistress of the
Graces. The statue wants that elegant ease and
evident symmetry of parts which compel instan-
taneous homage on the part of him who looks on
the Venus de Medici.

If the traveller has any love for the horrible,
he will visit the Museum of Natural History,
where, besides an excellent collection of minerals,
stuffed birds, and anatomical preparations in wax,
he will find the celebrated representations of the
Plague, by the Sicilian Abbate Zumbo. They
form, indeed, a ghastly exhibition. In the same
building, a room has been fitted up in honour of
Galileo, with statues of him and other famous
men, and frescoes illustrative of his discoveries.
One cannot help thinking, in such a place, of that
sad chapter in Italian history which narrates the
sufferings of the great philosopher, whom priestly
ignorance buried in a loathsome gaol, because he
discovered one of the grand truths of nature.

In a back street of Florence still stands the

Buonarotti palace, owned by the descendant of the great sculptor, and in the sacristy of the Church of St. Lorenzo are several statues by that master of the art. Adjoining this apartment, you see the Chapel of the Medici, an octagon, encrusted with valuable marbles and siliceous stones, the splendid mausoleum of Tuscany's most celebrated princes.

We spent one evening in the Church of Santa Croce, the Pantheon where lie the ashes of so many mighty dead;

> —— " dust which is
> Even in itself an immortality."

Externally this place of worship possesses every characteristic of ugliness; but close to the entrance on the right, your attention becomes fixed on the tomb of Michael Angelo, a sarcophagus, over which Painting, Architecture and Sculpture mourn their loss, with a bust of the great Tuscan, executed by his own hand. Next it a far nobler monument has been erected to the memory of Dante, who sits in a meditative attitude above, while Italy and Poesy weep for the departed, and the former points to an inscription, " Onorate l'Altissima Poeta."

Then you come to Canova's famous work in honour of Alfieri, opposite to which a humble marble marks the spot where Galileo's ashes wait the sound of the trumpet which shall wake the slumberers of the tomb.

The Casine, or Hyde-park of the Tuscan capital, is a long, narrow plantation of tall trees on the banks of the Arno, below the city. Here, on a summer evening, the fashionables assemble to drive their curricles, and listen to the Austrian regimental bands. Pony chaises appeared "the rage" during our stay; and I was surprised to see the Florentine noblemen imitating the fast men of England, who build private stage-coaches and drive four-in-hand.

The avenue on the Arno looked like the road to Epsom, with this exception, that I did not observe one rider who could sit his horse. The equestrian exhibitions which we witnessed on the part of the Austrian officers, both at Milan and Florence, were really ridiculous. In the former town, we one evening passed a crowd busily engaged in jeering two young Germans, one of whom had fallen off his charger, while the other, attempting to assist his comrade, seemed unable to move without inflicting on his horse such punishment with his spurs as no animal could bear. By-and-by, his military cap fell off; a bystander picked it up; in bending forward to receive it, he again wounded the steed; but by this time the discomfited man had remounted, and away went both cavaliers down the Corso Orientale, looking like two John Gilpins, whose career would speedily end, the mob meanwhile raising a shout of derisive laughter at the expense of "i Tedeschi." If the Austrians succeed in retaining Hungary, it is to be hoped that the Magyars, who, like the English, love their horses and equestrian exercise, will teach them how to ride.

The first evening on which we drove in the Casine was one of those lovely ones which can only be enjoyed in a southern clime: a refreshing breeze rustled the foliage overhead, a flood of light had fallen on the wooded hills on each side of the Arno, and the setting sun gilded with a radiance almost tropical the lofty Campanile of Florence.

This belfry, a quadrangular edifice, 260 feet high, cased with marbles of different colours, and certainly the most exquisite building of the kind in Italy, stands close to the cathedral of Santa Maria del Fiore, in the centre of the city. The church itself is a vast building, presenting a singular appearance on account of the variegated marbles with which its outward walls are faced. Behind the high altar is Michael Angelo's last and unfinished work, Christ taken down from the Cross, with a suitable inscription by Cosmo III. Whilst we were in the cathedral one day, the municipality, guarded by soldiers and preceded by the Tuscan colours, entered to attend mass. "Who is that marching in front?" I asked. "That," answered my neighbour, "is the Gonfaloniere." The Gonfaloniere of Florence! What memories does that word recal, what glorious chapters in the history

"Della bella Italia, ov' è la sede
Del valor vero e della vera fede."

The church of Sta. Maria del Fiore once witnessed another scene. On the twenty-sixth day of April, 1478, the brothers de Medici invited the dignitaries of the place to meet in that holy edifice Cardinal Riario, apostolic legate, charged with important communications from the Holy See. Scarcely had the officiating priest elevated the consecrated wafer when Francesco de Pazzi, the rival of the ruling family, rushed on Guiliano de Medici, and, assisted by a hired assassin, stabbed him in several places with his dagger: while Lorenzo was only saved from a like horrible death by the interposition of a friend. During this frightful scene, the Archbishop of Pisa was attempting to overpower the magistrates in the palace; but the resolute Gonfaloniere Cesari Petrucci was not a man to be awed by priestly villany: he seized the plotter, and soon afterwards hung him, in his prelatical robes, out of the windows of the mansion. Scarcely had the news of this dastardly revolt reached the citizens of Florence when they flew to arms in favour of Lorenzo de Medici, and insisted upon the immediate execution of the ruffians who had threatened him and killed his brother.

Thus ended one of the foulest conspiracies recorded in history, a conspiracy which, though aided by the Pazzi, was planned by no less a personage than Sixtus IV. Pope of Rome, who employed as his principal agents his nephew Riario, and Salviati, the Archbishop of Pisa, and, as their subordinates, a strong body of ecclesiastics, devoted to the interests of the papacy. In this instance, at least, if not in others, he whom misguided men believe to be the Vicar of God on earth, the perfect representative of Deity, was, in plain terms, a murderer. And yet scholars of the present age tell us that through this wicked man, as well as through Alexander the adulterer and Leo the infidel, the virtue of a true succession has descended from the apostles of our Lord. Well may Chillingworth, while writing about this extraordinary delusion, call it a belief " cousin-german to the impossible."

One of the most interesting objects in Florence is the Laurentian library, begun by Lorenzo de Medici, and enriched by his various successors, till at length, in 1532, Leo X. issued a bull directing Michael Angelo to design an edifice suitable to contain so splendid a collection of manuscripts. A very polite custodier showed me, in this celebrated room, a copy of Virgil which has descended from the remotest times; one of the Koran, also of ancient date; and, amongst others, beautifully illustrated editions of Juvenal, Cicero, Homer, Dante, Petrarch, and Boccaccio, executed in the fifteenth century.

The churches in Florence, not even excepting that of Santa Maria Novella, which Buonarotti called his " sposa," are unfinished, their façades being almost invariably of rough unhewn stones, having a most repulsive appearance. Report ascribes this peculiarity to the pecuniary caution of the citizens, who wish to save to their exchequer the customary sum which the Pope expects to receive on the completion of every place of worship. The admirers of Salvator Rosa and M. Angelo Caravaggio will find some very fine works by those great masters in the palace of the Corsini family overlooking the Arno.

The principal square in the Tuscan capital is one of the handsomest in Italy. The Post-office occupies one side, and the Loggia, or open gallery of sculpture, another; the latter adorned by Judith and Holofernes in bronze by Donnatello, Cellini's beautiful representation of Perseus carrying Medusa's head, the Rape of the Sabines, and other works of art. Crossing a lateral street, you enter the old Ducal Palace by a gate, on either side of which are Rossi's Hercules and that colossal statue of David which M. Angelo in his early years carved out of a large piece of marble spoiled by a preceding artist. The great hall of the building contains large frescoes, representing the most famous actions of the Florentine republic; and above the square rises that beautiful tower erected by Arnofo, which you see in every engraving of the Tuscan capital, and which certainly must be considered one of the most graceful of the architectural ornaments of Italy.

Adjoining this ancient seat of democratic dignity an immense gallery, designed by Vasari in the sixteenth century, extends to the Arno, occupying the upper story of the houses on both sides of a street, which a bridge connects at the end next the river. It contains the invaluable collection of sculpture, paintings, bronzes, monuments, and gems, presented by the late Archduke Leopold to the nation. Statues, chiefly Grecian, fill the corridors, among which a wild boar, evidently a very ancient relic, particularly attracted my attention.

Two large rooms are devoted to portraits of paint-ers, chiefly their own handiwork; others display a vast variety of specimens of the Venetian, French, Flemish, Dutch, and Tuscan schools; and at the end of the third lobby has been placed Bandinelli's copy of the Laocoon.

I might fill pages with descriptions of the pic-tures of Guido, Guercino, Vandyke, &c., well known to artists as forming the attractions of this collection; but let me close these brief allusions to the

> " Matchless gems of Art's exhaustless mines,"

which are treasured up in the " Athens of Italy," by mentioning the room called the " Tribuna," which contains the pearls of great price. On pe-destals in the centre of this little apartment stand the Grinder, the Wrestlers, the Apollo, those noble remains of ancient Greece; and, last of all, the inimitable Venus de Medici, which throws Canova's " magnum opus" quite into the shade. Byron has summed up the excellencies of this statue when he says,—

> " The goddess loves in stone, and fills
> The air around with beauty."

c 2 .

Ranking with the Laocoon and the Apollo Belvidere, both in the Vatican, it has as yet never been equalled by modern art; nor has Thorwaldsen himself succeeded in copying that spirit which lives and breathes in every Athenian statue.

Whoever desires to enrich his home with works of Italian art, should visit my friend Signor Petrini, Borgo Ognissante, and the studios of the other painters and sculptors, whose copies of celebrated masterpieces will give pleasure to their possessors in after years.

For the first few days of our stay in Florence, the *table d'hôte* had been but poorly attended. One afternoon, however, on descending to the *salle à manger*, I found covers laid for a large party. Turning to a waiter, I asked the reason of the altered appearance of the table; with difficulty able to restrain his laughter, he replied, " Why, this morning, Sir, we received a whole colony of Americans, fourteen travelling in one party, and several smaller ones." The words were scarcely out of his mouth when the door opened, and in marched an army of men, all upwards of six feet high, dressed in suits of black, and conversing about the

" lions " of the city with the nasal twang so peculiar to people of a certain rank of life in their country. We met them afterwards in various public places, and with all their peculiarities, for none of them belonged to the aristocracy of the Great Republic, they were agreeable intelligent men. Among the shopkeepers of the United States, there is quite a mania for seeing Europe; every man who can scrape together five-hundred dollars, goes off to visit the cradle of the arts, spends his all on his tour, and returns to make more.

This class of people, and the numerous commercial travellers sent by American merchants to arrange mercantile affairs both in Britain and on the Continent, living as they do always in the best hotels, and travelling in the most expensive manner, produce an unfavourable impression respecting the manners of their countrymen on the minds of Englishmen, who, totally ignorant of the state of society across the Atlantic, set down every man from the United States whom they may chance to meet, as a specimen of the upper classes. This is not only unjust, but excessively foolish. No person who has mixed even for a few days in the best society of Boston, New York, Philadelphia, Baltimore and Charleston, does not know that an American gentleman is as much a gentleman as any squire in England, and that the ladies will advantageously compare at least with a great majority of their sisters in the fatherland. It is the universal diffusion of education which has covered the older countries of Europe with American travellers in the lower walks of life, and those countrymen of ours who dislike their manners should not forget that the same class in England scarcely know where Italy is, and if they were carried thither, like Orlando, on winged chargers, would behave with a good deal more vulgarity than their Transatlantic neighbours. I have heard American tradesmen criticising works of art, and alluding to historical incidents during visits to various European countries, in a manner that would make some even of the squirearchy of England hide their diminished heads.

On the evening of the last day we spent in Florence, a thunder-storm passed over the city, attended by heavy rain, hail, and the fall of large pieces of ice, which, besides driving beneath cover

the coquetting flower-girls and importunate cab-
men, threatened to break the windows of our
dwelling. It lasted, however, but a short time;
the heavy cloud soon passed away to swell the
streams among the Apennines; the streets resumed
their active bustling appearance, and the blue sky
of Italy reappeared, giving promise of sunshine on
the morrow.

CHAPTER III.

ONCE every three years, a grand illumination and
festival take place at Pisa, in honour of St. Ranieri,
patron of the city. On this occasion strangers
from all parts of Tuscany, and even from the adjoining states, flock thither to spend a night in
merriment and masquerading. The occurrences

which happened at the celebration of 1851,—the projected plot against the Austrian government, the arrest of two gentlemen professing to be sons of an English peer, and the consequent excitement, are familiar to every reader of the newspapers.

I left Florence by railroad on this well-known holiday, not however for Pisa, because such plea-sure-seeking crowds accord not with my taste, but for the Eternal City, to witness the processions of Corpus Domini. We had started from the quay Lungho d'Arno in the diligence which proceeds to Rome, taking advantage of the Strada Ferrata as far as Sienna. On reaching the handsome station near the Casine, the conductor showed us into a second-class carriage, built in the shape of a long car, precisely like those in the United States, and having accommodation for fifty people. The crowd on the platform was excessive, and not a little quarrelling ensued between guards and passengers respecting places. Already some forty-five gaily attired citizens had seated themselves in our car-riage, when a Frenchman looked in and asked if there were room. A unanimous shout answered " No;" but he, a true son of the " polite " nation, stepped boldly in, and pushing aside a lady, forced himself into a place. This rude conduct, of course, provoked the Italians present, and a violent altercation was the immediate result. However, " monsieur " retained his position, casting around him glances of scornful defiance, and squeezing the alarmed female beside him to make himself more comfortable. It was a lovely morning, the sun shining brightly on the valley of the Arno, and at every station we picked up a group of peasants attired in their best costume and bound for the grand " festa." I was exceedingly amused with an elderly burgher of Florence who sat opposite to me, and who seemed to be travelling on a railway for the first time in his life, for the motion, the bridges and embankments filled him with astonishment not unmixed with fear. The country, especially after the line crosses the river, is very pretty. On the hill-sides they were busy reaping the rye.

At Empoli, a place of some size, we left the crowded train of noisy merrymakers, and entering a carriage on a branch railroad, traversed flourishing vineyards and fields of maize as far as the finely situated town of Castelfiorentino. Beyond this, the soil being poorer, the crops appeared very light; much of the land too is underwood, peeping out of which every now and then you see picturesque villages, perched on the tops of eminences and surrounded by ancient walls. This railroad, with its long cars, and winding course up a wooded valley, the smell of the wood burnt by the locomotive, and the narrowness of the line, vividly recalled to my mind the scenery between Baltimore and Cumberland, on the route over the Alleghanies.

Passing through a long tunnel we reached Sienna, a strongly fortified place of twenty thousand inhabitants, built, it is supposed, on the crater of an extinct volcano, and celebrated for the purity with which its citizens speak the mellifluous language of Italy. A diligence was waiting for us at the station, in which we drove to the hotel, where travellers must dine, if they do not wish to be starved, for no further stoppage occurs until you reach Viterbo, fifty miles from Rome. For a long distance, after leaving this town, we passed over an uneven country with a sterile and badly tilled soil. Four horses, having a postilion to each pair, drew our vehicle, assisted by oxen at the steepest hills. Near Torrenieri, the bleak eminences reminded me of Spain, and San Pietro stands amid a plantation of olive-trees, exactly like those to be seen on the banks of the upper Guadalquiver.

The cold stiff soil around this place must have been the same referred to by the younger Pliny, when he remarks that some parts of Tuscany required nine ploughings, before the seed could be sown. We had hitherto occupied the coupé alone, but here we were joined by a Milanese gentleman, resident at Sienna, who had left his native city out of hatred to the Austrians. With him I had a great deal of conversation during the remainder of the journey, respecting the unfortunate state of Italy, and found him no republican, but willing to join with men of any principles, whose object was to expel the Austrians. He confirmed my impressions regarding the universal dislike felt by the people of Lombardy towards that military power, which, backed by the Czar, checks their enterprise, represses their mental activity, and attempts in every possible manner to reduce them to worse than Spartan slavery; but he, like his brethren,

looked for the good time coming; and when I expressed it as my opinion that the bayonets of
Hapsburg could not for ever crush the nations
between Hamburg and Sienna, between Mayence
and Belgrave, with vehemence he exclaimed,
" No, signor, i Tedeschi medesimi sanno che
questa tirannia non può durare; adesso siamo in
gran confusione, disjiunti e vinti, ma il tempo
per la vendetta verra." This gentleman had travelled in various parts of Europe, and spoke with
reverence of the constitution of England, but the
French character he despised. Their invasion of
Rome, he remarked, was quite consistent with the
former actions of a people whose fickleness and
want of principle had passed into a proverb. After
conversing for some time regarding the diplomacy
of the present age, and especially the manly conduct of Lord Palmerston in refusing to become,
like his predecessor, an Austrian policeman, or to
prop up governments which have rendered themselves despicable by their crimes, we adverted
to the peculiar position of the Romish Church,
whose weak vacillating head could not remain in
the Eternal City, unless surrounded by foreign

bayonets. I was struck by the effect which political
grievances had produced upon the mind of this
patriotic man. " I am a Roman Catholic," he
said, " but when I see the Pope leading the vanguard of despotism, indebted for his safety to the
bayonets of France, intriguing to garrison Rome
with Austrians, shedding the blood of his people,
and encouraging that treacherous Nero, the King
of Naples; when I look around and find Protestant
countries enterprising, happy and free, while Papal
countries are deserts like Spain, and trampled on
like my poor Italy; can you wonder, Sir, that I
begin to doubt the Divine origin of the faith of my
fathers ? "

Nothing can be more natural than this process
of reasoning; there are thousands in Italy, like my
eloquent friend Gavazzi, whose eyes late events
have opened; and I firmly believe that every
German detachment in that peninsula, every act
of persecution on the part of Neapolitan terrorists,
every tyrannical proclamation issued by Pio Nono,
every instance of martial law being inflicted in
Lombardy, add to the feeling which is rapidly
being diffused throughout Italy against the mon-

strous abuses of Romanism. When the dawn of
freedom first tinges the tops of the Apennines, woe
to the institutions of priestcraft! when the Croatian
dragoons cross the Tagliamento, a cry of " Down
with the Papacy!" will awaken the echoes of the
Quirinal Hill. Mazzini may be active, and his
party numerous; but the most efficient propa-
gandists of Protestantism and liberal principles are
the troops of Radetzky and the judges of Naples.

As we approached the higher hills, the country
became more desolate, but the moon rose in a
cloudless sky to light our way over the dreary
pass of Radicofani, 2,470 feet above the sea, and
bearing evident marks of volcanic action. A
wolf skulked across our path, as we descended
to the Pope's frontier at Pontecentino, where the
officers behaved much more handsomely than the
Austrians at Sesto Calende.

From Bolsena, the ancient Volsinium, once so
opulent that the Romans removed from it two
thousand statues, now a lonely deserted village,
we had a fine view of the lake, thirty-five miles
in circumference, which Pliny describes, and which
witnessed the triumphs of Roman arms two

hundred and seventy years before Christ. Every
traveller in Italy is familiar with the name of the
next town through which we passed, also situated on the banks of the " Lacus Volsiniensis,"
Montefiascone, celebrated for its wine. Whilst
toiling along the stony ill-kept road leading across
the plain between this place and the Voltumnian
hills, the conductor discovered, to his no small
consternation, that an iron bar, supporting the
drag, had got loose, and, twisting itself round the
axle, had driven a large hole into the " intérieur "
of the vehicle, besides cutting half through every
spoke of the wheel. But the Italians, unlike the
Spanish, soon effect the repairs necessary to enable
a disabled diligence to reach the nearest town, and
before nine in the morning we entered the ancient
town of Viterbo, pleasantly situated at the base
of Mons Ciminus, and surrounded by turreted
walls. We passed through its chief square just
as the municipal authorities, attended by French
soldiers, were marching in procession to mass
in honour of the Pope's birthday.

Having breakfasted on very poor fare, we began
to ascend the mountain, first between vineyards

and gardens, and then through a forest of brush-
wood. This hill might easily be cultivated.
The same soil in Scotland would have been
yielding heavy crops; but an indolent people and
a wretched government have conspired to arrest
all agricultural improvement in central Italy.
From the top we enjoyed an extensive view.
At our feet, surrounded by wooded eminences,
and said to have been the crater of an extinct
volcano, lay the Lake of Vico, whose waters,
tradition affirms, engulfed the city of Succinium;
on our right, beyond the desolate Campagna di
Roma, we saw the Mediterranean; and on our left
rose a few snowy peaks towering above the
Apennines.

Descending into an uninteresting valley, poorly
cultivated by peasants living in exceedingly dirty
villages, we crossed another elevation near Bac-
cano, and looked down on some parts of the
valley through which the Tiber flows. What
can that be which appears like a monument on
the shoulder of a hill some distance before us?
I asked myself the question without consideration,
but the next moment it flashed upon my mind

that the object to which my eyes were directed was none other but the cross which surmounts the stupendous dome of St. Peter's. We were travelling along the Cassian Way, the ancient high-road to Etruria, and at La Storta a postilion took charge of our diligence, who urged the horses into a gallop.

The sun was about to set beyond the eminences towards the west; its parting rays cast a flood of light on the houseless Campagna; far away on the slopes of the Apennines two white spots marked the sites of Tivoli and Preneste; a death-like stillness prevailed around us; not a tree waved over the road, not a bird sung in the fields; on one hand an ancient tomb threw a shadow across the highway to Veii, on the other the eye wandered helplessly over the deserted plain in search of a green object or a dwelling: all was desolate and lonely; but a feeling of breathless expectation silenced remark. We travelled rapidly, but uttered not a word; it seemed as if we approached the temple where the Goddess of Ruin dwelt, and trembled lest a word should conjure up the ghastly form of the divinity.

Before us was the Milvian Bridge, where Constantine saw in the heavens the vision of a cross, the emblem of truth, the antepast of victory; and a sweep of the road revealed a scene so different from the gloomy Campagna, that involuntarily I started, confounded by the sight, like the sailor who, dreaming of lowering clouds and heaving seas, awakens to behold the banana groves of the tropics. Recollections crowded into my mind. Thought succeeded thought too quickly to find expression; a host of the mighty dead seemed to pass across the stage, and the songs of triumphal warriors to die away on my ear, as at length alive to the reality of the scene before me, yet still awed by the deserted grandeur, the solemn royalty of Rome, I thought of earth's vicissitudes and of her whose glory has departed.

"The Niobe of Nations! there she stands,
    Childless and crownless, in her voiceless woe."

There are several commanding eminences, from which the stranger may obtain a bird's-eye view, both of the ancient monuments and of the modern edifices of imperial Rome,—the former peeping out amidst the gardens on the Esquiline, Palatine, and Aventine Hills, the latter occupying the level plain at a bend of the Tiber, called in former ages the Campus Martius. He lives perhaps in one of the numerous hotels or boarding-houses in and around the Piazza Spagna, a handsome square situated at the base of the Quirinal. As soon after his arrival as possible, let him walk down the Via Condotti, where cameos, columns, and Etruscan vases fill every shop-window, until he reach the Corso, a long bustling street which forms the great artery of the present city. " Can this be the ' lone mother of dead empires ?' this the decaying capital of the Cæsars ?" he exclaims, as he passes cafés crowded with French officers, walls on which placards, both in Italian and in English, announce the departure of steamers from Civita Vecchia, the publication of new guide-books, or the performance of a recent comedy at the theatre, the stylish equipages of British aristocracy, and the more lumbering coaches of the cardinals.

Surprised at the stirring appearance presented by a place which most people expect to find only venerable in its ruin, he turns to the left, and glancing at the Parisian-looking shops as he walks along, arrives at the Piazza del Popolo, an elegant open space, designed by Michael Angelo. An Egyptian obelisk, brought by Augustus from Hierapolis, with fountains and statues, adorns the centre of this square. The Via del Corso ends in two churches exactly similar in architecture, one on each side of the street, and opposite to them is the Porta del Popolo, so celebrated during the late republican struggle. Immediately overlooking this quarter of the city, and laid out as a fashionable promenade-ground, is the Pincian Hill.

Let us follow the carriage-road, which has been carried in curves to the top, for from no other point do the domes of the churches, and especially St. Peter's, appear so majestic. At the foot of this elevation, outside the walls, stood the Villa Borghese, embowered in beautiful foliage; but French cannon have rendered its site nearly as desolate as the Campagna beyond. The gardens of Sallust look down from the other slope of this eminence on the Campus Sceleratus, where the unfaithful vestals were buried alive.

Let us contemplate the scene from a different situation. We have found our way along the narrow intricate streets, crossed the river by the Fabrician Bridge and the island of the Tiber, formed, tradition says, by the wheat of Tarquin which the people threw into the stream further up, and which was here impeded in its progress; and, leaving the town by the Porta Portese, near which the stranger will be surprised to see a few little steamers, have driven along the walls as far as the Gate of Pancrazio, where blackened remains of villas, shattered mason-work, and injured plantations, bear witness to the conflict which raged so fiercely in that vicinity, between the French and the Roman patriots. Close to the bastion before us was the breach at which Oudinot entered, and at the top of the gardens attached to the Corsini Palace, within the ramparts, stands the house which Garibaldi occupied during the siege, and which was built on the site of Martial's villa. Scaffolding supports the half-ruined archway through which we pass to climb to the summit of the Janiculum, and the Church of St. Pietro in Montorio, the scene of St. Peter's crucifixion, once containing famous works of art, now almost destroyed by Gallic artillery. From this lofty elevation we can see distinctly the seven hills on which stood the ancient mistress of the world; notwithstanding the rubbish which has accumulated to a considerable depth in the interjacent valleys, and rendered the outlines of the eminences less marked than formerly. Very near this church, a noble fountain pours forth its liquid treasures into a basin so large, that boys use it for a bathing-place. Paul V. brought this stream from a distance of thirty-five miles. Refreshed by the coolness which it diffuses around, listening to the music of the falling waters, let us meditate on the changed fortunes of the city stretched out as in a panorama to our view.

We stand on the spot where Porsenna mustered his forces, and cast our eyes first towards the gardens amidst which the Coliseum rises like a feudal tower, then to the domes of Santa Maria della Maggiore and St. John Lateran, between us and the more distant Apennines, and lastly, towards the proud cupola which St. Peter's rears into the deep blue sky. Few cities in the world can compare with Rome in respect to the plenty and quality of the water conveyed to it. The Fonta Aqua Felice, built by Sixtus V., cools the air on the Monte Cavallo; the Fountain of Trevi, an immense basin with statues and artificial rocks, affords a plentiful supply to those who dwell near the college of the Propagande Fide, at the base of the Quirinal; and the Aqua Paolina at the top of the Janiculum, one of the most conspicuous objects in every view of the seven hills, descends to enrich the fountains of the Piazza San Pietro, and crosses the Sistine Bridge to benefit the city.

But to enjoy the prospect in all its grandeur, we shall ascend to the summit of St. Peter's, to the gilt ball which sparkles in the sunshine, four hundred and twenty-four feet above the pavement. The rays of heat have not yet acquired their meridian power; else we could with difficulty bear their intensity; but a flood of light nevertheless illumines the peaceful city. So far are we exalted, that the men and horses on the Piazza appear like Gulliver's Lilliputians, and the Tiber like a silver bow, whose string is the Via del Popolo. Our right hand rests on the Janiculum; our left reposes on the endless mason-work of the Vatican, and we look down on a maze of lofty houses, apparently without a plan, in the midst of which a break shows the site of the Piazza Navona, the market-place of Rome, where stands a beautiful obelisk found in the circus of Caracalla, and dedicated to Domitian. They sometimes lay this square under water by means of the gushing fountains in its midst; above it rises the cupola of St. Agnes. Could our eyes penetrate into the narrow streets of this quarter, we should see the cooks busily employed before their doors, undisturbed by passing carriages or cavaliers, and priests whose name is legion, hurrying to and fro, or gossiping with the citizens.

The inhabitants of Rome, especially the women, struck me, as a particularly fine-looking race; they dress too with taste and elegance, notwithstanding the inferiority of the shops; but beggars swarm, especially at the church doors. Nothing can exceed the filthy state of the suburbs; well may they be called " sentina gentium," the sink of nations. Yet the ancient city had a thorough system of drainage; travellers yet visit the remains of the Cloaca Maxima, or great sewer, begun by Tarquinius

Priscus, and completed by his son Superbus, which carried into the Tiber the waters of the Velabrum marsh, at the foot of the Palatine; and Agrippa, history tells us, performed a voyage in a boat through the drains, in order to superintend their repair; so complete, indeed, was the system adopted for the purification of the streets, that Pliny called Rome " the hanging city." But the Popes have not the public spirit even of the Tarquins; the Italians of the present day seem insensible to odours which would have filled with consternation the polite court of Augustus; the days of great undertakings have passed away, and perhaps the descendants of the she-wolf which nursed Rome's founder may yet find a den amid the ruins of the Capitol. One of the most imposing objects in the view from the cupola of St. Peter's, is Fort St. Angelo, "the Mole which Hadrian reared on high " for a place of sepulchre, deriving its modern name from a statue which surmounts it, representing the archangel Michael with his drawn sword. It was once faced with Parian marble; but not a slab of that covering now remains. Every reader of English poetry will recollect Byron's

vigorous denunciation of this structure, in which
he rates the imperial builder as a " colossal copy-
ist of deformity."   The effect produced by it
certainly excited different emotions in my mind,
and I am yet at a loss to know for what reason the
Castle of St. Angelo has not been regarded as one
of the most picturesque edifices in modern Rome.
As you pass between the gigantic statues on the
parapet of the Elian Bridge, which crosses the
Tiber at its gate, the seraph seems to brandish his
weapon over your head, and announce that he has
been sent from heaven to protect the Eternal City
against the infidel.

Looking beyond this isolated tomb, your eye
rests on the Pope's Palace, occupying the summit
of the Quirinal, now called Monte Cavallo, from
two colossal groups of men and horses, evidently
of Grecian workmanship, which surround the obelisk and fountain in the adjoining square.   Here
the Cardinals meet in conclave to elect a successor
to St. Peter, whom, when chosen, they proclaim
from a window overlooking the Piazza. More
distant still, the two towers of Santa Maria Mag-

giore may be seen, and quite across the city, at the
furthest wall, you distinguish the Basilic of St.
John Lateran. Turning slightly towards the south,
wandering for a minute over gardens and vineyards,
your glance soon settles on the Coliseum, " a ruin,
yet what a ruin! " the quarry to which palaces and
churches owe their stones; near it, the hoary wreck
of Cæsar's Palace crowns the Palatine; while to
the right, the pyramid of Caius Cestius marks the
spot where our countrymen lie buried. Perhaps
you may be able to discover the roof of the Temple
of Vesta, whose nineteen marble columns built by
Numa Pompilius still stand, attesting the excellence
of ancient Roman masonry, and forming one of the
most interesting monuments of distant ages which
time has not destroyed; or within a few yards of
this venerable relic, you may, if quick-sighted, remark the Ponte Rotto, the remains of a bridge,
the building of which Michael Angelo's rivals
succeeded in entrusting to another architect, although the great master had been promised the
work. Five years after its erection, according to
the prediction of the disappointed candidate for the

honour of constructing it, a flood carried away the insufficient arches, and but a wreck remains.

The greater part of the ground covered by the city in former times has now few inhabitants. There you wander among noble ruins enclosed in gardens and vineyards, whose manifold beauties delight the eye; days might you meditate on the Aventine, Cœlian and Palatine Mounts, among the groves of cypress and pomegranates, shaded from the fierce rays by o'erspreading fig-trees, and inhaling the perfume of a thousand flowers. The air of these solitudes is always laden with odours; the ivy twines on fallen columns; clusters of rich grapes hang from imperial archways, and bowers of roses seem placed there to invite meditation on the fate of empires, to cast a veil over the prostrate glories of a kingly race, and by the brilliance of their varied tints

> "To gild Destruction with a smile,
> And beautify Decay."

With what delight does your eye wander over the beautiful belt of pleasure-ground which with

its villas and wide-spreading foliage shuts out from
modern Rome the desolate treeless Campagna!
From the summit of St. Peter's dome you can trace
this girdle of gardens, beginning at the Pincian
Hill, and extending round the dwellings, till at
the Vatican it meets the shrubberies of the Pontiff.
Far in the distance you see the Apennines, with
Tivoli and Frascati, like white spots, on their
slopes; and the roads to these retreats you can
distinctly trace across the arid plain. What a
majestic prospect is that, whose different features
I have lightly traced; one could contemplate it for
hours, his mind wandering to far distant times,
when triumphal processions, on their way to the
temple of presiding Jove, carried the spoils of
eastern capitals,—when monarchs from the banks
of the Euphrates and the Danube laid their
crowns at the feet of conquering Cæsar; then
the proud eagle waved from the towers of that
palace on the Palatine, where the night-owl now
lurks in the ivy, and the falcon pursues its
quivering prey.

But we have not seen all; let us turn to the

other side of the stupendous dome, and look over
the Campagna to the dark blue sea. That
beautiful region, celebrated in the classics for the
fertility of its soil, has become a howling wilderness, where man has no dwelling, and malaria
forbids repose. Once the possession of an indus-
trious peasantry, who covered its valleys with
corn, its hills with vineyards, and its slopes with
useful woods, spared by Alaric, respected by the
Vandals, it became a spoil to the rapacious nobles
who strove for mastery in the Eternal City; now
the Colonna set fire to its forests,—again the
Orsini retaliated on the farms of their Ghibelline
foes, till the husbandman deserted the smouldering
ruins of his home, left his fields to the rank
vegetation of a southern clime, and his watercourses, impeded in their flow, to become deadly
morasses, the nurseries of plague. The sun shines
beneficently upon you as you traverse this dreary
solitude; but not a tree remains of those forests
which afforded a grateful shade to the thirsty soil;
ruined aqueducts speak of happier days, and long
matted grass obscures the sacred spots, where

sleep, in forgotten sepulchres, ten thousand heroes who bore the arms of Rome.

The mischief commenced by the nobles, and continued by the banditti, who prowled from watchtower to watchtower in medieval times in search of plunder, in hopes of meeting some whose ransom would delight their souls, has been consummated, confirmed, legalised by avaricious priests, under whose government the Papal States seem rapidly hastening to irretrievable ruin. Some attempt to account for this sad change from physical causes; but man is the culprit, and nature only carries on the work which his neglect and violence began. You walk out now on these steppes, and a sense of loneliness soon creeps over you; for there is neither tree nor shrub to relieve the eye, only downs and plaited grass and horrible morasses: you sit down on a stone to muse on mankind's folly, when a troop of horses gallop past, starting at the apparition of a human form. Perchance you may hear the tinkling of the goat-bells, or the whistling of the plovers calling to their mates; but a house, or branch, or field of waving corn, you need not hope for there ; the sun burns the blade of grass, the night winds howl amid the rocks, and the few wretched inhabitants, who inhale the miasma of the swamps, look, not like living breathing beings, but like spectres walking in their shrouds.

CHAPTER IV.

NOTES ON THE RUINS OF ROME.

INUNDATIONS OF THE TIBER—WHO DESTROYED THE MONUMENTS OF ANCIENT ROME?—RIENZI, LAST OF THE TRIBUNES—THE CITY IN THE FIFTEENTH CENTURY—CLIMATE OF CENTRAL ITALY—THE PANTHEON—COLUMNS OF MARCUS AURELIUS AND TRAJAN—BATHS OF TITUS, OF DIOCLETIAN, AND OF CARACALLA—THE APPIAN WAY—VALLEY OF EGERIA—TOMB OF CECILIA METELLA—THE CATACOMBS—ROAD TO TIVOLI—MONS SACER—THE CAPITOL AND TARPEIAN ROCK — THE FORUM ROMANUM — TEMPLE OF JUPITER TONANS—ARCH OF SEPTIMIUS SEVERUS—THE MAMMERTINE PRISON—THE COLISEUM—ARCHES OF TITUS AND CONSTANTINE—THE PALATINE MOUNT, ITS RUINS AND GARDENS.

ALL students of ancient Roman history will recollect how frequently the Tiber, swollen by heavy rains, or melting snows in the Apennines, overflowed its banks and carried away the buildings situated on the Campus Martius.* Augustus

---

* The following lines of Horace will, perhaps, revive the memories of school-days :—

"Vidimus

spent an enormous sum of money in clearing and widening its bed; indeed, few of the emperors were not forced to devote much of their attention to projects for preventing the periodical destruction caused by these inundations. The inhabitants of the modern city have however no occasion to dread the recurrence of such a catastrophe, for the rubbish and soil washed down from the adjacent hills, and the foundations of houses now destroyed, have raised the level of the plain about fifteen feet. Above-ground we yet behold some noble monuments of the days when every known region of Europe and half of Asia obeyed the mandates of the Cæsars; but under-ground there exists a vast quarry, the excavation of which may yet fill the antiquarian with joy. But who thus mutilated, shattered, and overthrew the edifices of the imperial city? Oh, the Goths and Vandals, you reply; like flights of locusts they issued from the forests of the north, crossed the Julian Alps, and busied themselves in applying the besom

"Vidimus flavum Tiberim, retortis
Littore Etrusco violenter undis,
Ire dejectum monumenta Regis
Templaque Vestæ."

of destruction to the architectural triumphs of Italy.
The answer may be plausible; but it is not true.
Spoilers of a different kind had the greatest share
in the work of demolition.

"The Roman nobility," says Mr. Hallam,*
"not content with their own fortified palaces,
turned the sacred monuments of antiquity into
strongholds, and consummated the destruction
of time and conquest. At no period has the city
endured such irreparable injuries; nor was the
downfall of the Western empire so fatal to its
capital as the contemptible feuds of the Orsini and
Colonna families."

Kings too had a share in the devastation.
We are told that Charlemagne decorated his
palace at Aix la Chapelle with marbles from
Rome; and many centuries afterwards Robert
of Sicily employed vessels in transporting to his
dominions the slabs and pillars of temples found
on the seven hills. "Itaque nunc, heu dolor!"
Petrarch indignantly exclaims, "heu scelus in-
dignum! de vestris marmoreis columnis, de limi-
nibus templorum (ad quæ nuper ex orbe toto

---

* History of the Middle Ages, vol. i. p. 279.

concursus devotissimus fiebat), de imaginibus sepulchrorum sub quibus patrum vestrorum venerabilis civis erat, ut reliquas sileam, desidiosa Neapolis adornatur. Sic paullatim ruinæ ipsæ deficiunt." In another passage of his works the laureate remarks that " the citizens have done with the battering ram, what the Punic hero could not accomplish with his sword."

The example thus set by nobles and princes was closely followed by several Pontiffs of the Church. Pope Gregory I. waged war with the temples and statues found within the walls, he burnt the library on the Palatine, and anathematized all who dared to admire the vestiges of former greatness. That rude Franciscan, Sixtus V., adopted a similar course of procedure. "Clear away these ugly antiquities," he replied to the remonstrances of a more enlightened Cardinal; he totally destroyed the Septizonium of Severus, and threatened to blow up the Capitol if the Grecian statues were not taken away. Had death not happily removed the barbarian from the scene of his havoc, the tomb of Cecilia Metella would have been reduced to a shapeless mass of ruins; and as it is, he pulled down some of the noblest relics of the Augustan age to build the tasteless palace of the Lateran.

In those days every one regarded the ruins only as so many quarries, from which the nobles might erect their watch-towers, the peasants their farm offices, and the priests their sacred domes. The theatre of Marcellus was a stronghold, fortified by the Savelli; even the remains of the numerous temples which formerly covered the Aventine, have now disappeared, and columns, which once adorned the habitation of Capitoline Jove, now contribute to the great Church of St. Peter's. Even the shrines of Venus were desecrated to afford materials for the erection of Christian temples.

Near the ruins of the Palatine Bridge, adjoining that beautiful building which Servius Sullius dedicated to Fortuna Virilis, the stranger will find the house where dwelt Cola di Rienzi, last of the Roman tribunes. Byron calls him " The friend of Petrarch—hope of Italy," and he won the heart of the patriotic poet, by his stern denunciation of those aristocratical and priestly spoliators who rioted among the prostrate monuments of a greater age. There are few characters in history so romantic as that of him who revived for a little time the free institutions of a people whose virtue had been corrupted and whose spirit was gone. For a time "the fire of old Rome" seemed to have returned; but it blazed only for a moment, to expire in deeper gloom.

In the fifteenth century Rome was the abode of herdsmen; the elevations had been forsaken, and a few dwellings, huddled together along the river, alone indicated the site of the world's capital; morasses occupied the low ground, wild cattle fed on the eminences; the seat of Jupiter Tonans had become "the hill of the goats," and the Forum Romanum "the cows' field."

In the year 1443, Pope Eugenius IV. returned from Avignon to restore the glories of the "Eternal City," which his predecessors had deserted; but a considerable time after that happy event, Poggius thus moralises from his station on the Capitoline Hill: "Ut nunc omni decore nudata, prostrata jacet, instar gigantei cadaveris corrupti atque undique exesi. Consedimus in ipsis Tarpeiæ arcis ruinis, pone ingens portæ cujusdam, ut puto, templi, marmoreum limen, plurimasque passim confractas columnas, unde magna ex parte prospectus urbis patet, Capitolium adeo immutatum ut vineæ in senatorum subsellia successerint, stercorum ac purgamentorum receptaculum factum. Respice ad Palatinum montem— vasta rudera—cæteros colles perlustra, omnia vacua ædificiis, ruinis vineisque oppleta conspicies."*

While wandering amidst the ruins of ancient Rome, and meditating on those causes which contributed to make desolate the sites of buildings famed in a classic age, I found myself constantly repeating the expressive lines in Crabbe's ballad of Sir Eustace Grey,—

> "Vast ruins in the midst were spread,
>   Pillars and pediments sublime,
> Where the grey moss had form'd a bed,
>   And clothed the crumbling spoils of Time."

There is a brilliance in the climate of Central

---

* De Varietate Fortunæ.

Italy, which cheers even these solitudes. The gloom of a northern atmosphere would fill them with phantoms, the spectres of a vanished race, risen to avenge the desecration of their tombs; but in the rosy light of morn, or the more chastened rays of evening, you can admire the luxuriance of nature, amid the ruins of art, or the remains of fallen fanes and prostrate columns. You may breathe the fragrance of wall-flower, and gather the rich clusters of the vine, while the fig-tree shelters your bower, and the bright flowers of the pomegranate wave in a breeze, which seems, as if lulled by the loveliness of these gardens, to die away among the foliage.

I sometimes thought, while walking in the vineyards of the Aventine, that the scene might once more inspire the muse of Virgil, could he revisit the groves where Mæcenas patronised his rustic songs.

The first visit I paid in Rome was to the Pantheon. There is something sublime in a building which has stood 1878 years, and formed a temple for the worship of Jesus, as well as of the

divinities of a heathen age. Akenside, in one of
his odes, graphically describes it as standing

> " Amid the toys of idle state,
>   How simply, how severely great."

No excessive ornament detracts from the erect
grandeur of this venerable dome; it seems old
and frail, but shows no signs of dissolution. Like
an aged patriarch, who has lived contented and
frugally, it bears the marks of time, but preserves
the vigour of youth. Centuries have rolled away
since its noble portico first received the worshippers
of the gods; but these columns bid fair even yet
to survive the fall of modern monuments. In the
neighbouring Piazza Colonna stands the column of
Marcus Aurelius, raised by the senate to com-
memorate his German victories. It is one hundred
and twenty-eight feet high,—only four feet lower
than the still more beautiful pillar in the Forum
of Trajan, which celebrates that emperor's victories
over the Dacians. The bas-reliefs on these columns have served as models to sculptors in all
ages; those on the latter represent 2,500 male

figures, besides animals, chariots, &c. The splendour of the workmanship has not yet been equalled by modern art, but remains in the presence of incredulous men, to attest the high civilization of the empire.

The thermæ of Rome were originally designed for baths; but in process of time had gardens, theatres, museums, and libraries added to them, —in fact, became public lounges. Titus erected those bearing his name above the palace of Nero, the rooms of which are now subterranean. An old guide conducts the stranger through these spacious chambers, and, exalting a torch on a pole, shows him the remains of fresco paintings, whose colours have defied the efforts of. time. So beautiful are they, that Raffaelle copied from them several of his designs for the Loggie of the Vatican. On the summit of the Esquiline, now used as magazines for hay and barracks for French soldiers, are the enormous thermæ of Diocletian, covering an enclosure upwards of 4,000 feet in circuit; they afforded room for 3,200 bathers. But by far the grandest ruins are those of the Baths of Caracalla, situated among beautiful vineyards

in the Appian Way. Several of the Mosaic pavements have been well preserved, and the arches
struck me as of extraordinary span. The guide
conducted us, in due form, to the apartments where
were the hot, cold, and vapour baths, the swim-
ming-halls, the library, robing-room, theatre, and
many other chambers of vast size, still majestic
in their decay, though huge fragments have fallen
from the roof, and lie on the marble floors. Many
of the finest statues were found when they cleared
away the rubbish from this enormous edifice.
The gigantic walls, the extent of the rooms, and
the height of the porticoes, impress one with
respect for the grandeur of conception displayed
by the Romans, even during the declining days
of the empire.

Between the Flaminian Way and the Tiber,
completely blocked up by, and indeed forming the
support of houses, you will experience great difficulty in finding the Mausoleum of Augustus, a
lofty circular building, exactly similar to the
Castle of St. Angelo. A considerable portion of
it still remains, but so hidden by the dwellings of
one of the most densely-peopled parts of the city,

that you may pass close to it frequently without observing its moss-covered walls.

Of all the drives around Rome, none pleased me so much as that along the Appian Way. For a mile or two we passed between gardens shaded by the leaves of the fig-tree, adorned by the scarlet flowers of the pomegranate, and watered by little courses which the aqueducts supply. In the coolness of evening, when a mellowed light tinges the Apennines, and a gentle breeze refreshes the heated air, how delicious slowly to pursue one's way between the imposing ruins of Caracalla's Baths and the more modest tombs of the Scipios, passing through the Arch of Drusus to survey the remains of the aqueduct which Claudius formed to supply this part of the ancient city; and then, leaving the walls by the Gate of St. Sebastian, to meditate, during eventide, in the fields of that very Valley of Egeria where Numa Pompilius received from the goddess all his laws respecting the arts of peace and the worship of the divinities! Let us descend from our carriage to the vineyards which now cover that sacred spot, and return to wonder at the vast Circus of

Romulus, 1,700 feet long, by 260 broad, over-looked by

"A stern round tower of other days,"—

the lofty tomb which contains the ashes of Cecilia Metella, and forms one of the most interesting remnants of antiquity within the territories of the Papal See. On the other side of the Appian Way from this ivy-covered monument, you observe a small unpretending church, almost hidden by foliage. It belongs to the indigent monks of St. Francis d'Assisi, and constitutes one of the seven basilics of Rome; for under it are the Catacombs, the subterranean galleries in the rock where the persecuted Christians worshipped, and buried their dead. Tradition tells us, that fourteen popes and 170,000 Nazarenes there lie interred. We entered the open door of the place of worship, and pulled a bell communicating with the adjacent monastery. By-and-by a careworn, miserable man appeared, dressed in the scanty garments of the brotherhood; and, handing candles to each of us, led the way down to the gloomy corridors, where Peter is said to have declared the unsearchable riches of Christ.

Will the reader follow me now in another direction? Ascending the Monte Cavallo, we pass between the gardens of Sallust and the Esquiline, and, driving through the Porta Salaria, the same by which Alaric entered in triumph, visit the Villa Albani, to see Rafael Mengs' beautiful fresco of Apollo and Mnemosyne on Parnassus with the Muses. Then we turn to the left, and join the road which leads from the Porta Pia, by the Villa Torlonia and church of St. Agnes, across the Campagna to Tivoli. Gradually we leave behind us the vineyards and gardens which form a belt round the city, and enter the desolate downs on the banks of the Anio, where, in a little rounded eminence, solitary as the ocean, we recognise Mons Sacer, famous for the secessions of the Roman plebeians, the scene of Menenius Agrippa's fabulous exhortations. But we are now a long way from the Piazza Spagna; the sun has set behind St. Peter's; and in these southern regions we must bear in mind that no twilight befriends the wanderer, but, soon as the orb of day has declined in the western horizon, "the shadows fall," the stars rush out, and "at one stride comes the dark."

But we have yet by far the most interesting part of the ruins to survey. We shall, for this purpose, ascend to the top of the Capitol, and stand on the brink of the celebrated Tarpeian Rock, " the promontory whence the Traitor's-leap cured all ambition." Its height has been much lessened by rubbish accumulated below; but still no one would exactly choose to cast himself from its summit into the gardens beneath it. We look down upon the ancient Forum, known to every schoolboy from his earliest years. It occupies the low ground between the Capitoline and Palatine Hills, and around it stood the Senate-house, the Comitium, and other buildings famous in the classics.

Immediately at the foot of the rock on which we have taken our position, are three splendid isolated Corinthian columns, supporting a sculptured frieze of beautiful workmanship. This constitutes all that remains of the temple of Jupiter Tonans. Close to it eight Ionic pillars of Egyptian granite, forty feet high, and all of different diameter, indicate the site of the Temple of Fortune; while a little to the left the arch of Septimius Severus, raised by the " senatus populusque," commemorates the victories gained by that emperor in the East. This highly decorated monument is in excellent preservation. Within a few yards of its archway, a narrow stair descends into the sub-terranean cavern, formerly called the Mamertine prison, built by Ancus Martius, and rendered more famous, in after times, by the tradition that the apostles Peter and Paul were there confined, under Nero.* Here we put our hands into the cavity in the rock, said to have been caused by St. Peter's head, (!) and drank of the stream of water used at the baptism of Processus and Mar-tinian, the keepers of the dungeon, whom their prisoners converted from heathen error to the truth as it is in Jesus.

The single column of Phocas stands by itself, at the side of the Via Sacra, so called from the sacrifices which accompanied the peace between Romulus and Tatius. It commences at the Coli-seum, passes the temples of Romulus and Remus, the splendid remains of the temple of Sesostris,

* The classical scholar will recollect that Jugurtha, Zenobia, the confederates of Catiline, and other illustrious prisoners, were likewise confined in this dungeon.

the nine columns of the temple of Antoninus and Faustina, the Curia Hostilia, the Basilic of Constantine, and the beautiful arch of Titus, and enters at the Fabian gate the Roman Forum. This cluster of noble ruins has been often described, and as often represented in engravings. There was the heart of the ancient city, and from thence emanated laws which were obeyed from the Euphrates to the Pillars of Hercules, from the Danube to the Mountains of Mauritania, and the Cataracts of the Nile. The moderns have deserted this splendid site, to build on the plain below; and if Poggius could resume his musings on the Palatine, he would still see only desolation, and mourn over decay.

Let us now, holding our breath—for the magnitude of the building oppresses our feelings—enter the great amphitheatre of Titus, the wonderful Coliseum,—" an edifice," says Gibbon,* " which, had it been left to time and nature, might perhaps have claimed an eternal duration."

Every one knows the history and uses of this famous structure. Having been converted into a

---

* Decline and Fall of the Roman Empire, vol. viii. p. 456.

fortress by the Frangipani and Anibaldi during
the days of aristocratic feuds, it suffered much
from the hands of violence; but still it stands
unequalled in the wide world as a relic of the past.
It had a triple row of arcades, raised one above
another, and each consisting of eighty arches.
The form is oval, the height 157 feet, the circumference more than one-third of a mile; on its
benches 87,000 people could be accommodated,
while 20,000 more stood on the terrace above.
These figures give some idea of its vastness; but
the bird's-eye view from the highest tier exceeds
all description; and when the moonbeams shine
through the ruined gateways, the effect mocks the
power of language. To the well-known stanzas
in the fourth canto of " Childe Harold " the
reader must refer for by far the most graphic
written account of this stupendous edifice, and
the feelings which it produces in a susceptible
mind.

You sit on a crumbling bench of stone, and
listen to the moaning of the wind as it passes
through the arches: can this be the suppressed
roar of the African lion, or is it the last exclama-

tion of the gladiator who has been carried out to die?—the sigh, perhaps, of some holy martyr to the faith once delivered to the saints, who has been sacrificed to gratify the brutal passions of a people thirsting for that sort of excitement which calls loudly for blood. You cast a hurried glance down to the arena, almost expecting to see the wild beast seize his victim; or up to the regal box, where Caligula smiled as the tigers tore out the hearts of his fellow-men;—you feel mentally transported to those rude days, and can scarcely realize the pleasant fact, that now no one appears on that once cruel stage but the Christian stranger, who execrates the sports of Rome.

Between the Cælian and the Palatine hills stands the Arch of Constantine, consisting of three arcades, eight Corinthian columns, and several bas-reliefs in excellent preservation. To adorn this edifice, the subservient senate, after the defeat of Maxentius, stripped many of the figures off the Pillar of Trajan, thus mutilating an old monument to disfigure a new; for what can be more out of place than Parthian captives at the feet of an emperor who never encountered that nation, and the head of Trajan placed on the body of one of Constantine's enemies? This trophy remains a monument of senatorial syco-phancy and artistic decay.

I conclude this brief sketch of a few of those venerable ruins which have attracted strangers of all nations to Rome, by asking my reader to return with me once more to the Appian Way, and enter-ing a vineyard by a little door, climb to the sum-mit of the Palatine, to enjoy the splendid prospect of the seven hills, which presents itself from the Palace of the Cæsars. Three thousand columns once adorned an edifice whose crumbling walls now form lurking-places for the birds of night—in whose saloons the gardener cultivates his vege-tables—and whose towers are crowned with ever-green oaks, and cased by entwining ivy. Here Nero held his bacchanalian orgies—hither Augus-tus invited learned men—within these halls Cali-gula devised new schemes of bloodshed. How splendid were the apartments in these days of Roman power! and they are beautiful still; true, the gold and purple have vanished, the menials have ceased to attend in the vestibule; the pageantry of the court is no more; but perhaps few spots in Europe can compare, in point of romantic loveliness, with the groves of oak, the cypress thickets, and the bowers of jessamine, which mingle with the ruins on the Palatine.

CHAPTER V.

Two or three miles down the Tiber stands the Basilic of St. Paul, originally erected by Constan-

tine over the cemetery where, according to tradition, the Apostle of the Gentiles was buried. A
fire in 1823 consumed the greater part of this
edifice, which is now being rebuilt in a style of
splendour perhaps unequalled in Europe. Eighty-
eight columns of the finest Carrara marble support
a roof resplendent with gold, and the walls will,
when finished, be faced with the same material.
The cost of the undertaking—an extravagant one,
considering the financial condition of the country
— has yet to be ascertained, but it must be
enormous.

Near the Porta Maggiore, built by the Emperor
Claudius to carry his noble aqueduct over the
roads to Labicum and Preneste, the stranger will
find the Basilic of Santa Croce, which contains a
large portion of the holy cross found by St. Helena
in Jerusalem, some of our Saviour's thorns, and
other relics, to doubt the authenticity of which,
would be considered the direst heresy. Prostrate
before the case enclosing these trumpery fabrications, may generally be seen some deluded votaries,
whose uplifted hands, and rapt expressions, testify
how firmly they believe in the sanctity of the place
dedicated to the accursed tree.

The Basilic of Santa Maria Maggiore, the chief church in Christendom over which the Virgin presides, stands on the top of the Esquiline hill, and appears conspicuously in most views of the city. The chapels of the Holy Sacrament and the Borghese family are rich with gilding and jewels, but few men of taste will admire either the external architecture, or the internal decoration, of this structure.

We arrived in Rome shortly before the feast of Corpus Domini, and first entered St. Peter's, to hear the chanting at vespers on the preceding evening. Most people are familiar with the general appearance and situation of that august temple, which took 150 years to complete, and is perhaps the most wonderful display of architectural vastness in Christendom. It stands on the slope of the Vatican hill, looking over the Tiber and the houses of the modern city towards the Quirinal. The way to it leads through narrow streets, inhabited by an indigent population. Suddenly emerging from them, we found ourselves in the Piazza St. Pietro, a spacious ellipsis, upwards of 1,000 feet in length, having on each side four

rows of columns, which support a balustrade forming the pedestal of 192 statues. In the centre
stands an Egyptian obelisk, brought from Heli-
opolis, and two handsome fountains.

In common with many others, I must confess
my disappointment with the first view of St.
Peter's. It affords a remarkable instance of how
much the effect of vastness of dimension may be
lessened by variety of architecture; you cannot
realize the sublimity of *the whole*, for *the parts*
divert your attention, whether you will or not.
Is this the church, you say, which excels all
others in magnitude, on which Michael Angelo,
Raffaelle, Bramante, and Bernini, exercised their
powers? But when you begin to compare the
statues, or pillars, with the stature of living men,
—when you have time, one by one, to study the
details of the building,—its colossal proportions
stand out, as it were, in greater relief, the littleness
of surrounding objects becomes more visible; and
as your eye wanders from the flight of steps leading to the great door, to the figures above the
façade, and from thence upwards to the summit
of the stupendous dome, you feel growing upon

your mind that impression of the gigantic which the stranger generally bears with him to his distant home.

To the architecture of the front few will become reconciled; I never looked at it without lamenting that Bramante did not live to carry out that plan which St. Gallo and Maderni have so barbarously altered; but the dome appears more and more sublime on every successive visit. Gazing on the gilded ball which surmounts the giant cupola, your mind seems to dilate, till, forgetting the insignificance of earthly things, you rise to the full understanding of the shrine before you; the proportions of the edifice expand as you carefully contemplate them; gradually feelings too rare for ordinary expression banish every sense of disappointment, and a reverential awe creeps over you, produced by immensity, and similar to that experienced by the visitor to Chamouni, when, three hours after the sun has set behind the hill of Forclaz, he beholds it illuminating the snows on the summit of Mont Blanc.

Some writers estimate that St. Peter's cost twelve millions sterling. With what important consequences was this outlay fraught to the nations of the world! Little did Bramante and Michael Angelo think, when they projected this vast work, that the sale of indulgences to defray its expenses would bring about a mighty reformation of the Romish Church. The Pope reared a monument which forms the wonder of succeeding ages; but in doing so, he gave the signal to Martin Luther to begin that war which ended in the triumph of Protestantism among the most energetic nations of Europe. This unexpected result may prove to us, that a greater than Rome's Pontiff is the Head of the Christian Church; that the worldly wisdom of Leo was purposely turned into folly by Him who sitteth on the circle of the Heavens, and confounds the designs of the proud.

The thirteen gigantic statues above the façade of St. Peter's, represent our Saviour and his twelve apostles; you can walk on the flat roof beside them, and survey the proportions of that dome which rises four hundred and twenty-four feet above the pavement. The interior, which forms a Latin cross, is divided by Corinthian pillars into three naves; under the high altar you descend a few steps to the tomb of St. Peter, and Canova's celebrated statue of Pius VI; looking upwards from which you behold the top of the cupola, with the inscription in large letters on its frieze: " Tu es Petrus, et super hanc Petram ædificabo ecclesiam meam, et tibi dabo claves regni cœlorum." Who has not heard of the tombs which decorate the principal church of Christendom? A pyramid of white marble in relief, near the entrance door, the work of Canova, marks the final resting-place of the last three of the Stuarts; and Thorwaldsen has a noble monument to Pius VII.; but the piece of sculpture which pleased me most, was Canova's beautiful tribute to the memory of Clement XIII. Above the Pope appears praying, at one side Religion holds the cross, and at the other you see the Genius of Death; while two bas-relief lions, symbolic of the Pontiff's strength of character, recline with Charity and Fortitude below. During vespers on the eve of Corpus Christi, for half-an-hour I laboured under the delusion that one of these figures was alive. To describe in detail the architectural ornaments, or the internal decorations of the church, would be out of place in a work like the present;

the curious will find them minutely examined in the books of abler travellers, whose pens can do justice to their merits.

Let me invite the attention of my readers to the scene which I witnessed in the Piazza, and at the altar of St. Peter's, on the great feast of Corpus Domini. The day broke cloudless and serene, and the sun of Italy rose in all its splendour, to illuminate the procession of dignitaries. Early in the morning I joined the vast crowd, which flowed like a resistless river towards the Vatican. The broad way between the rows of pillars on the Piazza, was strewn with box-wood leaves and fine yellow sand, and along this path, shortly after our arrival, the ecclesiastics began to march in order towards the cathedral. A very courteous officer in charge having provided us with front seats along the line, we saw the spectacle to great advantage. The French soldiers had scarcely taken their positions to keep back the multitude, when the students for the ministry appeared, forming the vanguard of the various orders of monks, whose coarse garments, rope girdles, and sandals, strikingly contrasted with the rich dresses of the ladies around us. Behind them walked the priests and singing boys, two abreast, each man carrying a lighted candle, the wax from which dropped plentifully on the sand. I never saw in any country such an array of dirty, vulgar, ignorant looking men; the regulars, especially, had a most repulsive aspect. At intervals amongst the clergy, porters with tattered robes carried gilt crucifixes, and the standards of the several saints, followed by the bishops, the archbishops, and the bearded patriarchs of the Greek and Armenian churches in communion with Rome. After them came the cardinals, headed by Antonelli, the famous prime-minister of the Holy See—generally speaking, handsome elderly men, with intellectual countenances. They preceded a sort of throne, covered by a canopy, and borne on men's shoulders, on which, his head and shoulders only being visible above the robes of state, reclined Pope Pius IX. He looked downwards, and as he passed very slowly, I had time to remark his careworn countenance, and the anxious glances which he cast from side to side, as if somewhat suspicious of his faithful Romans. He has grizzly hair, an expression by no means intellectual, and a face not nearly so venerable as those of the more aged cardinals.

Immediately behind Pio Nono, rode General Gemeau and his staff, taking precedence of the Roman nobles, led by Il Principe Altieri, a body of very handsome, elegantly dressed men, who constitute the Pope's guard of honour. How humiliating to them to see their place usurped by Gallic officers, to whom their Pontiff owes his restoration and his safe residence in the Eternal City! The heavy Norman cavalry followed, and the other horse regiments of France brought up the rear of the procession. As soon as they passed, we hastened to the sacristy door, and entered St. Peter's a few minutes before the Pope from the High Altar gave his benediction to a prostrate people. It was a solemn moment. The old man having descended from his throne, mounted the steps, and turning towards the assembled thousands, raised his hands. Immediately the vast multitude fell on their knees; looking over the forest of heads, I could see no upright figures but those of a few Inglesi and Americani, the nations who enjoy great liberty of a certain kind in Rome.

I have been in churches abroad where no such profanation would be allowed, where the Protestant must bow the knee or be punished; but the attitude of the strangers in St. Peter's, even on that sacred occasion, seemed to excite no attention whatever; every man did what was right in his own eyes. Exemption from conforming to the rites of popery has been purchased in the Eternal City by English gold. It is NOT necessary in Rome to follow the customs of the Romans. The bearing of the people during the ceremony was respectful, but scarcely devout; they seemed to favour the religion, but to bear no good-will towards its ministers. As for the French soldiers, they behaved with great levity; when a particularly fat monk passed, one man touched another with his musket, and an audible titter along the ranks stopped the paternoster of the unfortunate padre, who gazed mournfully on the scoffers.

We remained for some time in the Piazza, when the crowd had begun to disperse, in order to see the equipages of the cardinals, the heavy coaches with gilt ornaments, red wheels, and black horses, which are so numerous in Rome. Three footmen generally stand behind, while a stout coachman in a gorgeous livery sits on the hammer-cloth. The splendour of the vestments worn by the ecclesiastics did not come up to my expectations; the standards, too, bore marks of age, and many of the clergy seemed sadly to want soap and water. It was a childish procession, the offspring of " Night's daughter, Ignorance;" the vain effort of minds darkened by superstition, to honour that "God who is a Spirit, and must be worshipped in spirit and in truth." If religion consist in prostrations, holding wax-candles, and what Dr. Chalmers calls " a gurgle of syllables," then Rome is its capital; if men be rational beings, and their God accept only the offerings of the heart, then the mystery of iniquity works on the seven hills, and Rome is the Babylon of prophecy.

On the evening of the following Sunday half the people of the city flocked to the Piazza of the Lateran Church, to witness the procession of the Holy Sacrament. The Basilic of St. John's stands on elevated ground, close to the southern walls. A splendid obelisk, brought by Constantine from Thebes, adorns the adjoining square, and near it is a small chapel, with a portico covering the staircase, belonging to Pontius Pilate's palace at Jerusalem, up which Our Saviour walked to meet the governor.

All readers of history know the Scala Santa, which the faithful ascend on their knees. Whilst watching the deluded beings so engaged, I thought of Luther's visit to the place, and the flash of light which there revealed to him the mummeries of Antichrist. We found the vast open space in front of the church filled with citizens, soldiers, and carriages. The procession left the Basilic by a side door, made a circuit to pass through an hospital, and entered again by the great door of the eastern front. Several hundred priests and singers, the various orders of monks, the students of divinity, men carrying crucifixes, flags, and the emblems of different saints, preceded the cardinals, and behind marched a company or two of French infantry. There is something of a deeply melancholy character in this frivolity. No man, who has read his Bible, can gaze with indifference upon a multitude of immortal beings, whose religion of bodily exercises pleases the eye, but does not affect the heart. Methought I heard a voice from heaven, addressing these devotees of crucifixes and gilt images in the solemn words with which Isaiah, at the bidding of the Lord of Hosts, warned the rulers of Sodom and the people of Gomorrah.*

Two days after this we again mixed with a crowd of sightseers in the Piazza of the Lateran, to celebrate the festival of St. John the Baptist. I stood for an hour at the porch, watching the carriages of the princes and cardinals as they drove up to the entrance; and shortly before the appointed time a body of dragoons at full gallop announced the approach of Pio Nono, who followed them in a carriage, drawn by six horses. He sat at the window, bowing graciously to the people, and looking much more cheerful than he had done during the procession of Corpus Domini. Then entering the church, being dressed in black, I was admitted within the space railed off for the higher ecclesiastics and the officers of the French Republic. The fantastically dressed Swiss guards kept order, while the Pope, elevated on a chair,

* Isaiah i. 10—17.

was borne on men's shoulders to his throne. He was attired in his most gorgeous robes, wore a tiara glittering with jewels, and ever and anon stretched out his hand to bless the kneeling multitude. His countenance struck me as that of a man without much talent, but easy-minded and benevolent, apt to be misled by evil coun- sellors, but naturally disposed to gentleness. When he had taken his place on the pontifical throne, the cardinals one by one ascended the steps, bowed to him and kissed his hand—some of them with great apparent reverence, others as if they were performing an unpleasant duty.

This ceremony being over, the Archbishop proceeded to the altar to celebrate mass; but I did not remain, being sick at heart of such pomp and parading—in honour too of one who was among the lowliest of Christ's followers. How corrupted and changed is the church, how much has it departed from the example of Him, whose advent was announced by a voice, crying in the wilderness, " Prepare ye the way of the Lord!"

Within the Vatican is a little chapel, well known to all strangers, especially to those who have spent

the Christmas holidays in Rome. It contains
Michael Angelo's celebrated fresco of the Last
Judgment, on which the great master worked
for about eight years. Many of the figures in
this wonderful undertaking illustrate most forcibly
the grandness of outline and the boldness of
conception, for which he was so famous; but the
painting as a whole is not a pleasing one; it
justifies, in my opinion, Salvator Rosa's satire,

> " Michel Angielo mio, no parlo in gioco
>   Questo che dipingete è un gran Giudizio',
>   Ma, del giudizio voi n'avete poco."

A man's head, with ass's ears, in this fresco, was
meant for a portrait of the Pope's master of
ceremonies, who had ventured to decry the work
as unsuitable to the Cistine Chapel. The representation of the Deluge on the roof is interesting,
on account of being the first which M. Angelo
painted on plaster. In the other decorations of
this place of worship he only spent twenty months,
—an incredibly short time when we consider the
number of compositions, chiefly illustrative of
scriptural subjects, executed by his unaided hand.
When Julius II. wanted him to ornament them

with gold, in order to give splendour to the chapel, he replied, "In those days gold was not worn, and the characters I have painted were neither rich nor desirous of wealth, but holy men, with whom gold was an object of contempt." *

The appearance of the Vatican itself,—that immense palace which Guide-books say has eleven thousand rooms,—reminded me of Rasselas' dwelling in the Happy Valley. "This house," says Dr. Johnson, "which was so large as to be fully known to none but some ancient officers, who successively inherited the secrets of the place, was built as if Suspicion itself had dictated the plan." † It adjoins St. Peter's, and is connected with Fort St. Angelo by a covered passage above the houses. Having been added to and altered to suit the tastes of various pontiffs, its architecture is a piece of patchwork, which rather disfigures the locality, and detracts from the majestic appearance of the neighbouring dome.

Every stranger must visit with great pleasure the beautiful galleries, so well known to admirers

* Vasari's " Vite dei Pittori."
† Rasselas, p. 4.

of Raffaelle's genius.   On the ceiling of the Loggie,
under Leo X., he painted fifty-two scenes from
scriptural history, called on that account his
" Bible."   To the worthies of the Old Testament
times, he in these inestimable frescoes has given,
to borrow an expression from Coleridge,

"Such seeming substance, that they almost live."

The picture of Joseph interpreting Pharaoh's dream
would be sufficient of itself to exalt Raffaelle to the
first place among painters ; then there are Moses
saved from the Nile, the Judgment of Solomon,
the Nativity, the Baptism of Christ, and the Last
Supper, where the moment has been chosen when
Jesus announces to the disciples " One of you shall
betray me."

I might fill several pages in briefly noticing this
wonderful monument of artistic genius, the store-
house from which students have, for three hundred
years, been acquiring knowledge.   Raffaelle descended to the subterranean chambers of Nero's
palace to study the remains of ancient Rome ;
alone he remained, torch in hand, breathing the
damp air of vaults uninhabited by man ; but

there, perchance, the mantle of inspiration fell on his shoulders, he had recovered the manner of the ancients, the tastes which monks had buried under the ruins of learning; he could now connect the antique with the natural, the eternal and the true; and ascending to open day he painted his Parnassus, Apollo on Helicon with the Muses, to prove the resurrection of the arts.

To describe those glorious works of art, which attract so many strangers to the capital of Christendom, would be a pleasant task, but one which the reader will not expect of me. Before concluding these observations I wish, however, to notice a very few of those which cannot be mentioned without enthusiasm. A brief account of the treasures to be seen in the public as well as the numerous private galleries, fills many pages in every Guide-book; we paid considerably more than a hundred visits ourselves in Rome; but I would not venture to record my impressions of them here. Let me confine my remarks to six statues, and the chief works of four great painters hitherto not mentioned in the course of these remarks.

In the Spada palace, at the foot of the

Janiculum, those who, like myself, place Guercino in the first rank of painters, will find three works by him which leave a lasting impression on the mind—the Death of Dido, Mary Magdalene, and David with Goliath's head; but to see them you must pass through an ante-room, in which stands that very statue of Pompey, at the feet of which fell Cæsar pierced with wounds. A glance at this venerable relic answers the doubts which some have expressed regarding its authenticity. That stern face bears no resemblance to the handsome countenance of Augustus, or the boyish features of Alexander the Great; it tells its own tale to every reader of Roman history, and verifies the precious tradition. The presence of Pompey's majestic form fills the mind with sensations not easy to describe.

The church of St. Pietro in Vincoli, so called because built by Eudoxia, the wife of Valentinian, for the purpose of preserving the chains with which Herod bound St. Peter, contains Michael Angelo's celebrated statue, executed to embellish the tomb of Pope Julius II., and representing Moses with the two tables of the law. Of all the works which have immortalized this great sculptor, this example of creative genius impressed me most with admiration of his powers. You have there in marble the history and character of the Jewish lawgiver; you almost expect to see him dash in pieces the records written by Deity, and call aloud for the Levites to range themselves under the banner of the Lord.

Compared with the Quirinal, the Palatine, or the Janiculum, the Capitoline Hill is by no means a conspicuous object in most views of Rome. On the spot formerly occupied by the Temple of Jupiter — the summit of the rock — stands the Church of Santa Maria d'Aracœli; the equestrian statue of Marcus Aurelius, found near the Lateran, has been placed in the centre of the square, and the balustrades of the stair leading to the top of the hill are flanked with the various buildings of the Senatorial Palace, designed by Michael Angelo, which contains very celebrated collections of pictures, inscriptions, busts, and statues. The greatest ornament of the gallery is Domenichino's Cumæan Sybil, one of the best paintings which that master has left as a legacy to posterity. In the halls of the Conservatori the curious will find a representation, in bronze, found at the base of the Palatine, of the she-wolf which nursed Romulus and Remus; the same described by Virgil in the lines—

> " Geminos huic ubera circum
> Ludere pendentes pueros, et lambere matrem
> Impavidos." *

But, to my taste, the most wonderful work there preserved is the Dying Gladiator, a Grecian sculpture, which bears triumphant witness that, in one respect at least, modern must yield to ancient art. The attitude and expression of that inanimate marble can scarcely be imagined, even by those who have studied the master-pieces of a recent age.

Although I have inspected many collections of statuary in the various countries of Europe, I freely confess my ignorance of what could really be done by the chisel, until I saw that splendid range of apartments, filled with Grecian sculpture, which astonishes every visitor to the Vatican.

To mention by name the chief treasures of these halls would be tedious. Surely, Mr. Ruskin himself must allow that Perseus, with Medusa's

* Æneid, viii. 631.

head, and the Boxers, contained in the first
cabinet of the court, have immortalized the talents
of Canova; but let me not tarry to admire even
these; for the third circular room demands my
notice—the room in which Leo X. placed the
famous Laöcoon, discovered in 1508 amid the ruins
of the Baths of Titus, occupying the position which
Pliny has assigned to it, and described by the Venetian ambassadors in the time of Pope Adrian
the Sixth, in the expressive words, "Non gli
manca che lo spirito,"—nothing is wanting to it
but life. Two venomous serpents have entwined
themselves around an old man and his two sons,
one of whom endeavours, with his little arm, to
withdraw his leg from the tormentor; but, finding
himself unable to save the limb, he turns weeping
towards his father; the other young man seems
more resigned—every hope of safety has fled—the
intensity of the suffering has paralysed him. The
agony and despairing resolution blended in the
parent's face, divert your attention from the extraordinary muscular exertion displayed by his limbs,
as he summons a last mighty effort to escape the
fangs of the reptiles. But all will be in vain. As

you gaze on the features of the afflicted men, you expect every moment to see their strength fail, and their bodies, falling prostrate on the earth, become a prey to the devourer.

"Laöcoon," says Winckelmann, in his "History of Art among the Ancients," "nous offre le spectacle de la nature humaine dans le plus grand douleur dont elle soit susceptible, sous l'image d'un homme qui tâche de rassembler contre elle toute la force de l'esprit. Tandis que l'excès de la souffrance enfle les muscles, et tire violemment les nerfs, le courage se montre sur le front gonflé; la poitrine s'élève avec peine par le nécessité de la respiration, qui est également contrainte par le silence que la force de l'âme impose à la douleur qu'elle voudrait étouffer."

The same peculiarity has been remarked by Alison in one of his essays. As the agonies of his body increase, his mind seems to rise with the occasion, and no indication of defeat passes across his unconquerable brow. Truly has Byron illustrated the leading characteristic of this noble work, when he speaks of "Laöcoon's torture dignifying pain." The spirit triumphs over its woes; Nature

asserts, even in that horrible hour, the pre-
eminence of man. The contemplation of this match-
less monument of Grecian sculpture strikes the
beholder mute with astonishment; its presence
awes the frivolous, silences the prattler, and fills
with unspeakable admiration one who can justly
appreciate the majesty of art. No existent statue
can be named in the same breath with this, excepting perhaps that which the next chamber contains—
the Apollo Belvedere, discovered at Antium, and
pronounced by some judges to be the finest in the
world. " The god of life, and poesy, and light,"
erect, triumphant, and radiant with joy, stretches
forth his hand, as it were, to proclaim his mission,
while his attitude sets off the symmetry of his
form, and his look compels the homage which
mortals owe to Deity—the Deity which, amid the
groves of Delphi, established his awful oracle.

I have only mentioned Guercino. His admirers
must visit the spacious palace of the Colonna
family to see his Guardian Angel and his Moses
with the Tables of the Law; nor must they forget
among the various attractions of the Palazzo Doria,
to observe the Prodigal Son, the St. Peter, the St.

Agnes, the Magdalene, and the Endymion, which
his genius has added to the possessions of one of
the noblest Roman families. The mansion of the
Corsini, at the foot of the Janiculum, contains
three Ecce Homos, placed in juxtaposition, that
visitors may compare their merits. In Guido's,
resignation seems to predominate over every other
feeling; suffering is written on Carlo Dolci's; but
agony of the intensest kind cries in that of Guercino, "My God, my God, why hast thou forsaken
me?"

In the Church of Santa Maria degli Angeli,
once the Pinacotheca of Diocletian's Baths, now
belonging to the monks of St. Bernard, the stranger
will find Domenichino's masterpiece, "The Mar-
tyrdom of St. Sebastian," where that painter
proves himself a true disciple of the Caracci,
though greater than his lord.

All the world have heard of Guido's Beatrice
Cenci—the saddest of sad remembrances—which
adorns the Barberini Palace on the Quirinal hill;
but the lovers of true colouring will not object to
follow me also to the mansion of the Rospigliosi,
adjoining the Pope's residence on the same emi-

nence, where, in a pavilion of the garden, they will unexpectedly find the finest fresco which the world has ever seen—the celebrated Aurora, by that great master of Italian art. Apollo, seated in a car, drawn by four horses abreast, and surrounded by seven nymphs, representing the hours, is starting from a lofty promontory overlooking the sea, while the dawn of day illumines the landscape, and diffuses over the waters a rosy joyful light, to gladden the heart of the mariner dreaming of darkness among the breakers.

Let me conclude this imperfect sketch of the Eternal City by noticing one room in the picture gallery of the Vatican. Entering by the Loggie, and a narrow crooked passage, you arrive at a small apartment, which contains only five paintings, but these five merit more than a casual remark. On the same wall as the entrance, hangs Domenichino's St. Jerome, where, carrying out the ideal of Agostino Caracci, he has produced a masterpiece which, in point both of grouping and of expression, excels every attempt of his teacher. St. Ephraim administers the sacrament to the dying man, whose arm St. Paolina bathes with tears; while a deacon holds the chalice, and an inferior officer kneeling presents the book.

Next this picture is the Coronation of the Virgin, executed by Raffaelle when a youth, bearing, especially in the countenances of the figures represented, the evident marks of genius, although the grouping strikes you as stiff and hard. Alongside of it hangs another on the same subject by his disciples. This appears so inferior in the presence of works done by the master himself, that you quickly turn away from it to admire the colouring of the Madonna de Foligno, one of Raffaelle's greatest artistic triumphs. Mary, with the Holy Infant in her arms, sits in the clouds; on the ground beneath her a cherub holds up a scroll; on the right stand John the Baptist and St. Francis; while on the left, the secretary of Julius II., with St. Jerome's hand placed on his head, kneels in adoration.

Need I tell the enlightened reader what picture occupies the fifth and last place in this celebrated apartment? Nearly four hundred years have passed away since the small town of Urbino gave birth to Raffaelle; but no work of art has since appeared to challenge comparison with the Transfiguration.

The scene represented does not exactly tally with the scriptural account; for Christ appears raised in the air, with Moses and Elias on each side, while the nine disciples at the foot, not of a mountain, but a mere knoll, listen to the father and sister of the demoniac boy, who chide them for their inability to effect a cure. In the midst of this group, you see St. Andrew pointing to the hill whither the All-powerful Healer has gone, and beneath a tree on the left Lorenzo and Giuliano de Medici on their knees adore the transfigured Christ. The last of his works—the noblest fruit of that industrious genius which electrified Italy, the most elaborate of those well-studied masterpieces which impart to his name a dignity unrivalled—this magnificent painting displays the highest excellency of sketching, of colouring, and of conception combined. Rubens would have made our Saviour the sun, from whose person dazzling light streamed upon the beholders; but Raffaelle illustrates the brightness of the glory, not by any such vulgar device, but by its effects on the three astonished disciples; one has cast himself on the ground, another staggers as he endeavours to withdraw his head, while the third covers with his hands those eyes which cannot look on Deity. The confusion of the Apostles when they find themselves unable to heal the demoniac child—the endeavour of Andrew to pacify the relations by a reference to the power of Jesus—the father, whose face displays the fury of a man victimised by impostors—and the calm heavenly repose depicted on the countenance of Him who sits on the clouds on the top of Tabor, fill your mind with sensations—themselves amply rewarding a journey to Rome. Behold the culminating point of those precocious talents, which had delighted old Pietro Perugino in his assistant boy! From Perugia he removed to Florence; from Florence Julius II. called him to Rome, and there, undazzled by the splendid patronage of pontiffs and admiring kings, he pursued a course of steadfast industry; cartoons, drawings, frescoes, oil pictures, the result of patient study, astonished the artists of Europe, and when, to crown his triumphant progress, the Transfiguration appeared, it seemed as if the confines of perfection had been reached; Raffaelle gathered himself to his fathers, and Rome, says Castiglione, seemed joyful no more.

What a change from the bustling Via del Corso to the stillness of the Campagna Romagna, a few paces beyond the Cavalleggieri gate! Five minutes after leaving the walls, on our way to Civita Vecchia, we had entered the region of desolation, where stacks of meadow hay atone for the absence of houses, and troops of young horses trample on the graves of the dead. I had never spent a happier time than the days devoted to visiting the antiquities, the galleries, and the shrines of Rome. St. Peter's seemed grander each time I beheld it, and new beauties became visible in the works of Guido and Raffaelle on every successive visit; but the monuments of ancient splendour gave me the greatest pleasure; and many a time I resolved, should health and leisure be granted me, to bend my steps once more towards these glorious ruins, to wander amidst the fallen fragments of Caracalla's baths, to sit musing on the benches of the Colosseum, and to trace the windings of the Tiber from the moss-covered battlements on the Palatine.

CHAPTER VI.

THAT unhappy portion of Italy, which yields temporal obedience to the Roman See, remains very much in the same state as that to which corrupt rulers reduced it during what Isaac Taylor calls "the dog-days of spiritual despotism."*
The gift which Pepin granted for the remission of his sins, and Constantine declared a perpetual

* Spiritual Despotism, p. 191.

sovereignty—whose possession Arnold of Brescia denounced as incompatible with the character of Christian ministers, even before superstition had settled into the thickest gloom, has been shamefully abused by the successors of St. Peter. "The maxims and effects of their temporal government," says Gibbon, "may be collected from the positive and comparative view of the arts and philosophy, the agriculture and trade, the wealth and population of the ecclesiastical state."* What measure of general benefit did the Popes ever confer on their subjects? Expensive churches, ostentatious buildings, they now and then erected, when their coffers were full, or money could be raised by the sale of pardons; but few even of enlightened Catholics will now deny that their states are worse governed than any part of Europe. Sometimes a pontiff, more benevolent and well-meaning than his predecessors, by a rare chance was elevated to the throne; but corruption had so eaten into the vitals of official morality that he seldom could effect any reform; he found the ecclesiastics thoroughly vicious, and, therefore,

* Decline and Fall of the Roman Empire, vol. viii. p. 436.

abandoned every hope of staying the progress of that disease, which has increased in virulence until the present time.

At about the close of the seventeenth century the Venetians sent an envoy extraordinary to the Holy See, and he sums up his account of the province in these emphatic words—" Desolated of her children, ruined in her agriculture, overwhelmed by extortions, and destitute of industry." In a similar strain writes a visitor some thirty years before : he laments the burdens with which the proprietors are borne down and driven from the country, the miserable condition of the peasantry, the absence of manufactures, and the illegal exactions of priestly harpies.

It is both curious and profitable to study the records of these ages, and read the pathetic lamentations over the state of the Papal dominions, which the language of Italy renders so tenderly expressive. "Oppressions, most holy father," exclaimed Cardinal Sacchetti to Alexander VII., "exceeding those inflicted on the Israelites in Egypt! People, not conquered by the sword, but subjected to the Holy See, either by their free accord or the donations of princes, are more inhumanly treated than the slaves in Syria and Africa."* To produce this lamentable result, ignorance had joined rapacity. Gregory XIII., desirous of growing more corn, cut down the forests, near Ostia, which preserved the salubrity of the air, and raised the port-dues of Ancona, in the vain hope of making the foreigner contribute more largely to his revenue, while in reality he drove him to other better governed lands. When first Urbino and then Ferrara were added to the territories of the church, Europe expected that prosperity might revisit its shores, and the popes recover from their financial difficulties; but these newly-acquired provinces only shared in the general adversity of the unfortunate lands, over which Innocent III., by fraud and robbery, first established the supremacy of the Roman See.

It would be needless to multiply testimonies regarding the deplorable condition, physical, moral, and religious, of those people, who have so long

* Dante says of the Popes in the 19th canto of the Inferno—
"I' userei parole ancor più gravi;
Chè la vostra avarizia il mondo attrista,
Calcando i buoni e sollevando i pravi."

been misgoverned by ignorant and rapacious ecclesiastical dignitaries.* Every educated Englishman knows it; every traveller in Italy mourns the spectacle of wretchedness, which spoils his enjoyment of scenery and sky; all acknowledge the misery, although some may dispute its cause. But must this desolation always be? " Time was, when to be a simple Roman was to be nobler than a northern king." Can the spell not then be broken? can the land where valour dwelt with wisdom not be disenchanted once more?

Two theories on this solemn subject occur to the mind. The age of ignorance has gone by,—feudalism no longer cramps the energies of nations, —intercourse, the press, and national commotions have quickened the activity of the mental powers even in countries oppressed by ecclesiastical and political despotism. Knowledge is fast disseminating itself throughout Italy, and, if it be true that endurance has a limit, that armies can never effectually triumph over exasperated men, and that

* " Illustrissimi et Reverendissimi Cardinali," exclaimed Bishop Bartholomew, the primate of Hungary, before the Council of Trent, "indigent illustrissima et reverendissima reformatione."

alliance with foreigners has shaken the confidence
of many in the infallibility of the Pope, then will
the Romans rise, and rise in arms, with irresistible
united strength, not to fall amid the ruins of the
Forum, but to destroy for ever the temporal power
of the Papacy.

Such is the hope of Italian patriotism.   It lies
nearest to the hearts of thousands now quiescent,
but biding their time; men who fondly cherish the
belief, that a senate will yet make laws in the
Capitol: but a vague, indeterminate, yet fixed
sentiment of a far different kind seems to fill the
minds of a less numerous class, visitors to rather
than natives of the peninsula.   They dream not of
revolutions or republican triumphs, but of earth-
quakes, blasting, and mildew; wandering along
the Campagna they hear subterranean wailings,
low murmuring sounds, symptoms of volcanic
agency, the foretaste, as they think, of those
terrible convulsions of the ground which, as
Vesuvius indicates, and the fate of Melfi proclaims,
will overthrow the works of ages, and announce
that the time has arrived when Rome, like Babylon, "swept by the besom of destruction," must

become " a possession for the bittern, and pools of water."

Perhaps there does not exist in the wide world a more disagreeable place than Civita Vecchia; the country around reminds one of Arabia rather than of Italy, and its narrow, dirty lanes emit a stream of odours altogether indescribable. I had spent a wearisome day there formerly, on my way from Naples,* just before the French bombardment of Rome, and now again necessity compelled me to remain for a few hours, waiting the departure of the Sardinian steamer bound for Leghorn.

Having endured a night of jolting on the execrable road between the Eternal City and its principal port, and assisted to extricate our diligence from deep sand, in which the wheels had become so firmly imbedded, that no efforts of the horses could move it, I was glad, on our arrival at Orlandi's ill-managed hotel, to enjoy a morning's rest. The forenoon proved insupportably hot, but towards afternoon a thunder-cloud from the

* For an account of Naples, see " Impressions of Central and Southern Europe." London : Longman & Co. 1850.

Mediterranean broke in torrents of rain over the landing-place.

One meets every now and then, when travelling on the continent, parties who think themselves fortunate in the possession of a carriage and a courier. "They are so convenient," say their owners; "we never have to complain of dirty diligences, or to take any trouble about passports, money, hotels, or modes of conveyance; wherever we go, post-horses can be procured, and François does everything for us."

An American merchant, whom we found on the deck of the packet at Civita Vecchia, described to me in words like these his comfortable manner of seeing Europe. "But," said I, "may I ask how much it costs you?" With all the *naïveté* of an inexperienced traveller, he frankly named a sum for each of his party per diem exactly three times more than I was paying. We had lived at the same hotels, visited the same places, and enjoyed the same luxuries; but he had scarcely come into contact with a single native, he knew nothing of the political state of the country, and Joseph, his "faithful" keeper, besides pilfering to an extent almost incredible, insisted upon his charge following the routes which he thought preferable.

Having myself crossed the Alps seven times by as many different passes, I gave this gentleman some hints regarding the best course to take on leaving Italy; "Oh yes, I see you are quite right," he replied; "that scheme has many advantages over the one adopted by my courier, but then he *must* have his own way; there is no good thwarting him." Certainly tastes differ; for what my friend considered travelling on pleasure, and a legitimate outlay of money, I should consider downright slavery and wasteful extravagance.

The case of this American must not be considered a solitary one; every summer many Englishmen thus commit themselves to the tender mercies of couriers, who rob them without scruple, and carry them just where they please. I once met abroad a person who engaged at Ostend or Antwerp an interpreter and servant, to assist him in making his way as far as Basle, along a route where every waiter, conductor, and steward speaks the language of our countrymen!

If a man does not take charge of his own affairs, he loses half the delight of travelling; in the public conveyances you meet people of all nations, whose conversation instructs and amuses; and while arranging the matters incidental to your progress, you get information beyond the reach of those who recline in Long Acre carriages, and trust to the management of couriers. Some of these men do act honourably; but the great majority are quite unworthy of confidence,—in league with second-class hotel-keepers, pledged to bring custom to friends, always on the alert to find excuses for an unnecessary outlay, and sure to make tourists feel as did Sir John Falstaff when he indignantly exclaimed,

"Shall I not take mine ease in mine inn?"

Freedom of commerce has rendered Leghorn the first port in the Mediterranean; mercantile men and captains of ships crowd its streets, and the canals which intersect it are filled with barges conveying goods to and fro between the vessels and the warehouses,

On the evening of the second day which we

spent there on this occasion, the procession of the
Holy Sacrament took place in the great square
adjoining the Cathedral.   Just before the appointed hour arrived the multitude showed symptoms of excitement: some rushed to the church,
and without any ostensible cause considerable confusion occurred; but in a few minutes a troop of
Croatian cavalry galloped into the Piazza with
drawn sabres, and in no very ceremonious manner
drove the people back on every hand.   Then
commenced the march of singers, priests, and
military, holding candles, and repeating prayers;
the Austrian band occupied the post of honour,
immediately behind the aged bishop who carried
the host; the German flag, too, floated from the governor's house, that black and yellow banner which
every Italian abhors, and which one day his nation
will trample in the dust.   Leghorn remains in a
state of siege!   And perhaps no city south of the
Alps more heartily execrates the Austrian name.
By quartering so many Croats there, the Duke of
Tuscany, some of the merchants assured me, has
for ever lost the respect of the inhabitants.

I have previously recorded my impressions both of this place and Pisa, distant by railroad about three quarters of an hour. Having spent some time in the beautiful Campo Santo of that city, admiring the Gothic arches, sarcophagi, and ancient frescoes which it contains, we drove out of the walls to a small wooden shed, purporting to be the station of the Strada Ferrata to Lucca. Much consultation took place among the clerks in regard to half a napoleon which I tendered as payment of our tickets; gold seemed to be quite a rarity to them.

Taking our seats in a long car with one fellow-passenger, who was reading an Italian translation of Quentin Durward, we were whirled along a plain well cultivated, densely peopled, and of great natural beauty. What a contrast to the Campagna of Rome! * Rows of willow-trees, on which the vines hung in graceful festoons, separated from

* Some of my readers may recollect with what pleasure Addison, during his Italian tour, observed the prosperous condition of the people in the small republic of San Marino; while the rich plain around Rome, the capital of civil and spiritual despotism, was desolate as newly-discovered wilds.

each other the fields of maize, beans, hemp, barley, and rye. The peasants were busy in some farms cutting down the barley in a peculiar manner, chopping off the ears separately, and afterwards removing the straw. In other fields the ripe and reaped corn was piled up under the trees, whilst oxen were preparing the ground for a second crop.

The walled town of Lucca stands in the centre of a pretty valley, surrounded by an amphitheatre of hills. Over the gate by which we sauntered into the streets, as if to mock a suffering country, appeared the word " Libertas," Austrian drummers meanwhile practising on the ramparts above! When passing along an unfrequented lane, I observed a picture placed on the walls, with three or four lamps before it, and a small altar with the following inscription, illustrative of that superstition which degrades the southern mind,—" Indulgenza di 40 giorni a che recitera 3 Ave Marias, by order of Monsignor Scali, Bishop of the diocese, and Legate of the Holy See." Such miserable chicanery scarcely requires remark; no wonder that licence prevails in Italy. The view from the ramparts and public drive of Lucca reminded me of that from the willows which weep over the ruins of Pompeii.

The locomotive which drew us back to Pisa, had on it a brass plate, inscribed, " W. Morris & Co. Philadelphia, U.S." What a commentary on the changes which a few years have brought about in the circumstances of nations! Time was when Christopher Colon wandered along the shores of the Gulf of Genoa, an energetic lad, full of the idea that a new world existed beyond the western waters, and that Providence had selected him to carry thither the civilizing arts; now Italy groans under two kinds of despotism, her manufactures have declined, her people have scarcely a place among the European powers; while a mighty republic from the banks of the Susquehanna and the Delaware sends works of industry to astonish her degenerate sons. Predominant among the flags in the harbour of Livorno, the stranger always finds the star-spangled banner: generally speaking, a large proportion of those who buy pictures and live in the best hotels hail from the Atlantic slope of America; and the eagles of Rome have deserted the Capitol on the Tiber, to inspire the Capitol on the Potomac with an energy which promises great things for the civilization of the world.

At the untimely hour of one o'clock in the morning we left Pisa by diligence to meet the Sardinian courier, — or *malleposte*, — at Pietra Santa, the frontier town of Tuscany. An avenue of chestnut-trees conducted us from this place to the douane station of the duchy of Massa and Carrara, a dependency belonging to Modena. A paul administered timeously to the officers of the "white eagle," saved us from a custom-house visitation here, as it had formerly done in the Eternal City. When on our arrival in Rome I opened my portmanteau to a handsomely dressed gentleman, whose fingers sparkled with jewels, he squeezed my arm significantly, and at the same time showed me clandestinely an open palm. The hint could not be misunderstood; I dropt a small silver coin into his hand, and my baggage was immediately declared exempt from the usual examination.

Under steep wooded hills, and commanding a fine view of the Mediterranean, stands the town of

Massa, whose eight thousand inhabitants are supported by the exportation of marble from the neighbouring quarries. The castle, a most picturesque object, occupies the top of a lofty rock, clothed with olive-trees; and when we passed the ducal palace in the chief square, the people were preparing to receive the ex-empress of Austria. Crossing a romantic dell by a bridge of white marble, we ascended the hills which separate the plains around the embouchure of the Arno from the valley of chestnut-trees, descending to which by a succession of zigzags, you reach the town of Carrara. Behind it rise three or four lofty mountains, picturesquely-shaped, but quite destitute of wood. They consist entirely of marble, the quarries of which may be seen a long way off. More than twelve hundred men work constantly in them, and the supply seems inexhaustible, for from these mountains they have never ceased to export marble since Romans there collected the materials to build the Pantheon.

.The beauty of the fields all the way from Pietra Santa to Spezzia must delight every traveller; they are carefully tilled, irrigated on the most scientific principles, and yield rich crops of maize, wheat, barley, rye, hemp, and beans, which the foliage of orange, lemon, fig, walnut, chestnut, and mulberry-trees, protect from the excessive heat of the sun. From stem to stem hang the festooned vines, their clusters almost meeting the heads of the Indian corn. As we passed they were busy cutting down the yellow grain, and ploughing the soil in preparation for the succeeding crop of vegetables.

In no part of Europe have I seen a district which had the appearance of more fertility, industry, plenty, and comfort, or which could with such propriety be taken as an illustration of the loveliness of that garden where our first parents dwelt before the fall. The smooth excellent road winds under the shade of trees forming arches overhead; you hear only the loud chirping of grasshoppers, and the ploughman's voice encouraging his team of oxen; agreeable odours rise from every field, and squalid poverty seems scarcely known.

Passing out of the little duchy into the territory of Sardinia, we stopped to lunch at Sarzana, an old city, which the Duke of Tuscany ceded to the Genoese in exchange for the then insignificant

Livorno. The road, on leaving it, crosses the Magra
river, which after floods devastates the entire plain.
We forded the first branch, and were transported
on a raft across the deeper channel; then we drove
for several miles up its right bank, and turning to
the left crossed a rising ground, from the top of
which we beheld the bright blue waters of the
Gulf of Spezzia, a calm lagoon among the hills,
overlooked by the houses of a pretty town. The
white lateen sails of the small craft lying in this,
the best roadstead on the Italian coast, had a beautiful effect, when seen peeping through the foliage
of the fig and the mulberry on the slopes of the
mountains.

A very steep ascent, presenting extensive views
of the picturesque coast, occurs immediately on
leaving this place; the road afterwards traces for
many miles the course of the river Vara, until at
Borghetto it turns sharply to the south, and crosses
two spurs of the Apennines—the first covered with
chestnuts, among which a few pretty villages are
embowered—the second becoming near its summit
rocky and bare, like the mountains between Malaga
and Granada in Spain. The people here seem

remarkably industrious; wherever soil can be found they cultivate it carefully, so that you see barley, rye, vines, and even wheat growing in spots which a Spaniard would have abandoned to red-legged partridges and stones.

We reached the top of the pass, and looked down from a giddy height on the sea, just as darkness began to brood over nature; and as we descended to Bracco,

"The fire-flies, swarming in the woodland shade,
    Sprung up like sparks, and twinkled round their way." *

When I roused myself next morning we had passed Cape Porto Fino, and were within a few miles of " Genova la Superba," and my former quarters at the Hotel des Quatre Nations. While referring to the political state of Sardinia, I may have occasion to mention the remarkable change which even two years of good government and active commerce have produced in the appearance of this city; meantime, let me pass on to notice the country between it and Nice.

Again seated in the *coupé* of the *malleposte*, we

* Southey's "Roderick, Last of the Goths."

traversed the long suburbs as far as the lighthouse, passing an incredible number of carts and wagons. For several miles beyond the rocky promontory, shutting out the view of the city on the west, indeed as far as the town of Sestri di Ponente, the road passes between a succession of villas, inns, shops, and rows of houses, forming, in fact, a *faubourg* to Genoa. Let not the stranger forget, when passing along the excessively narrow street of Cogoleto, that there Christopher Columbus first saw the light.

No description can convey an adequate idea of the beauties of this road to the mind of one who has never seen the cloudless sky, the luxuriant foliage, and the blue seas of Italy. Sometimes the way lies between gardens of figs and oranges, surrounding the villas, whose brightly painted walls peer out amid the foliage; sometimes you ascend a hill covered with chestnut-trees, wild myrtles, and olives, gaining from the top a noble view of the city of palaces, and the cliffs of Cape Porto Fino beyond; while below you the fishermen on the Mediterranean mend their nets, or impel their skiffs over the sapphire waves; at others you enter a large village surrounded with fertile fields, and supporting in comfort a thriving population.

A narrow cutting between rocks brought us to the picturesque town of Savona, where no fewer than three Roman Pontiffs were born. As darkness came on, the scenery was shrouded from our view; but myriads of fire-flies glistened around us, and ever and anon the revolving Pharos of Genoa poured a stream of brilliant light far over the Mediterranean. St. Remo, where we breakfasted on ripe figs, is one of the prettiest places on this romantic coast. It contains ten thousand inhabitants, who dwell in houses of great height, and, like the towns in the Grecian archipelago, has been built up the hill-side, instead of along the beach. The perfume of its orange groves is delicious; and even palms flourish in the neighbouring gardens.

Between Ventimiglia and Mentone, the road passes along the brink of frightful precipices, several hundred feet above the sea. To these succeeds another garden of oranges, and then a long ascent up a mountain, the summit of which presents a bold front of rock, while trees and vineyards clothe its slopes. Just under the naked

rocks, elevated some fifteen hundred or two thousand feet from the waters, and destitute of any
parapet, winds the road, and from it, so perpendicular is the declivity, you fancy you could leap
in one bound upon the deck of the steamer below.
I am not easily frightened, especially by the dangers of travelling, but stronger nerves than mine
would be required without a shudder to look over
that terrible precipice, as the heavy lumbering
diligence swings round the sharp turns of the road.
There are no descents on any of the Alpine passes,
not even on the Splugen, the Simplon, or the St.
Gothard, so difficult steadily and without tremor
to behold, as that above the little town of Monaca,
on this remarkable road.

One of the finest prospects in Europe bursts
upon the traveller on turning the shoulder of the
hill overlooking the ravine of the Paglion.   At his
feet lies Nice, with its lofty houses, castle, and
shipping, backed by a plain where mansions peep
out from an ocean of foliage; beyond, the promontory of Antibes stretches far into the Mediterranean,
and to the right rise, one above another, the frown-
ing mountains of Provence.

I shall not weary my readers with an account of this miniature Hastings—of the English villas near Cannes, or of that dirty seaport yclept Marseilles, which, although a Parisian assured me it required four days to see, we were glad to escape from in twenty-four hours. A large fleet, both of sailing vessels and steamers, fills its present harbour, which government has long ago found of too contracted dimensions for the wants of the shipping. A new port on the shore towards the west has been in process of construction for fifteen years; but fifteen years more at least will be required to finish it.

Acti labores sunt jucundi is a somewhat trite saying; but it applies with great aptness to the pleasures of travelling. To a mind well-stored with information and acquainted with the various incidents of European history, nothing can be more interesting than to visit the monuments of the Forum and the " blood-red fields of Spain ;" among the Alps, the Apennines and the Pyrenees, the lover of scenery will find Nature in all her grandeur arrayed; and those who know how delicious is the climate of the south will not wonder that Orientals imagine our countrymen under some potent spell, which, in the words of "Eothen," "drives them from their home like victims of the old Grecian furies, and forces them to travel over countries far and strange." But the delights of reminiscence must not be forgotten; memory imparts even to the fairest landscape lovelier hues, while it softens the sterner features of what at the time displeased; and you return from classic scenes to an island home, not indeed to erect a Parnassus, like that which Horace Walpole so wittily describes, but to wander, in recollection, again and again over those lovely regions, which the Mediterranean washes with its tideless waves.

CHAPTER VII.

NOTES ON THE POLITICAL CONDITION OF ITALY.

EFFECTS OF CLIMATE—THE NATIONAL CHARACTER—INFLUENCE OF DESPOTISM AND OF THE FINE ARTS—PICTURES AND CIVILIZATION —THE AUSTRIAN GOVERNMENT—ITS FINANCES AND SOLDIERY— OBSERVATIONS ON THE PRESENT STATE OF LOMBARDY, VENICE, TUSCANY, THE PAPAL TERRITORY, AND NAPLES—MR. GLADSTONE'S PAMPHLET—THE LAST OF THE BOURBONS—PIEDMONT AND SARDINIA—PROPHECY OF SIR E. BULWER LYTTON—PROSPERITY OF THAT KINGDOM—THE HOPES OF ITALY CENTRED IN TURIN—POLITICAL OPINIONS OF THE ITALIANS—THEIR CHOICE BETWEEN MILITARY TYRANNY AND REPUBLICANISM—INSTABILITY OF THE GOVERNMENTS NOW IN EXISTENCE—FEELINGS OF THE PEOPLE TOWARDS THE KING OF NAPLES—SPREAD OF DISAFFECTION TO THE PAPACY—PROSPECTS OF PROTESTANTISM.

"ITALIA, Italia ! O tu cui die la sorte
Dono infelice di bellezza, ond' hai
Funesta dote d' infiniti guai
Ch' en fronte scritte per gran doglia porte ;
Deh, fossi tu men bella, o almen piu forte."

THE motto from Filicaja, prefixed to this chapter, explains one of the numerous and complicated causes which have contributed to the degradation of a land, well described by Cooper, the American novelist, as " mighty in its recollections, but impotent in its actual condition." Tasso speaks of its delicious air, serene sky, beautiful trees and meadows, and charming waters ; * no doubt these natural attractions afford gratification to the traveller whose home is nearer the frozen sea, for to Italy flows a constant stream of valetudinarians, who seek a more genial climate, of persons interested in the relics of olden times, and of tourists, who wish to see with their own eyes the present state of a country, so favoured by nature and so celebrated in European history. But the advantages of situation, geological structure and soil, conferred with such profusion by Providence on this peninsula, have their drawbacks. The Neapolitan, whose olive-tree flourishes alike in the fertile valley or the rocky ridge,—in whose garden the Indian corn, watered by the streams from the Apennines, springs up with mushroom speed to fill his barns for months after harvest, has no stimulus to exertion, like that which rouses all the

---

* " V'e l'aura molle, e il ciel sereno, e lieti
    Gli alberi ed i prati, e pure e dolci l'onde."
                                        Gerusalemme Liberata.

energies of a German or a Briton; * *Dolce far niente* is the maxim for him; he bakes his *polenta*, basks in the sun, and lives the life of a vegetable.

Climate, south of the Alps, in some respects does the work which the farmer of the north does for himself; whilst in towns labourers may acquire, by a few weeks of active exertion, sufficient to fill their bellies during the remainder of the year. Warm clothing they can dispense with where frost and snow are unknown, and, except amongst the highest mountains, a frail covering of timber answers all the purposes of a house. An indolent temperament of body, every-one knows, generally produces a corresponding inertness of mind fatal to the best interests of a people. If an energetic patriot arise, he finds men affected by a languor which paralyses all his efforts to bring about a social or political reformation: the senses must be gratified, but the mind remain a blank; the theatre, the gaming-table, and the lounge, usurp that place which wise

* Seneca, de Ira, lib. ii. says: "Fere itaque imperia penes eos fuere populos, qui mitiore cœlo utuntur: in frigora septentrionemque vergentibus immansueta ingenia sunt, ut ait poëta, *suoque simillima cœlo.*"

men allot to the literary society, the workshop, and the schoolroom; education becomes universally neglected, because a livelihood can be earned without it; and philanthropic projects fall to the ground for want of men who will take the trouble to put them in execution. Had Italy enjoyed fewer of nature's bounties, perhaps her people would have at this moment occupied a very different position among the powers of the earth.

The national character presents a singular blending of somewhat incongruous materials. Quick in acquiring knowledge, excelled by none in discernment, eloquent from their birth, skilful in intrigue, and devoted to the beautiful, they are slaves to extremes of passion, though docile when not incensed by injury; eager to render their country the abode of empire, yet never able to devise well-ordered plans for its liberation; at one time you think you have found a clue to their inmost feelings, the next moment you find yourself deceived; like the tints of an autumnal sky, when clouds at sunset rest on the horizon, they present all the colours of the rainbow to the perplexed observer. A more philosophical review of past times might have performed miracles on behalf of the Italian people; but they have not learned aright the salutary lessons of adversity; blaming fate for what resulted very much from their own errors, they acknowledge neither the justice of the punishment, nor the wisdom of Him, who, when offended, showed Himself severe; they proclaim themselves entirely the victims of circumstances, forgetting those maxims of self-examination, which may be found in the writings of Plato, as well as in the oracles of God. If true to themselves, aware of their short-comings, and ready to profit by experience, they might even now have been triumphing over the oppressor.

But let us not be unjust, and, while assigning to the inhabitants of the Peninsula that portion of censure which they deserve, keep out of view the fact so justly stated by Mr. Whiteside,* that "the absolutism of the governments degrades the people, and tends to unfit them for political business." "It seems the height of injustice," says that accomplished writer, " to accuse men of ignorance and incompetence, when they are not suffered

* Italy in the Nineteenth Century.

to exercise their understandings, or show their ability for public life." The reasonableness of this remark will approve itself at once to every impartial mind, who knows how long a training men require before they can with safety be permitted to govern themselves. Even English jurisprudence has not been the birth of a day. Europe admires our senate house and courts of law, our freedom of speech and love of order; but these things have been the growth of time, the fruits of trial and error, the harvest of that seed sown by the barons on Runnymede, and watered by the Declaration of Rights.

No great work can be perfected without years of experience and development; and if a race are to be pronounced incapable of self-government, the verdict must be founded on the failure of a lengthened apprenticeship, not hastily given after centuries of oppression. If "domestic fury and fierce civil strife cumber all the parts of Italy,"* the blame does not wholly lie with the natives, but with those who have deprived them of the rights of citizenship, and of every privilege which ennobles man.

* Julius Cæsar.

Historians tell us of the Mogul Emperor Timour, who, after ravaging Asia by fire and sword, left pyramids of human heads, as so many holocausts on the altar of social order. Different, it may be, in degree, but similar in kind, are the measures which German princes have taken to overawe the injured inhabitants of the south; military law carries terror into the hearts of the Lombards, and Tuscany has become a barrack for Croats.

> "Italia ! thou art but a grave
> Where flowers luxuriate o'er the brave ;
> And Nature gives her treasures birth
> O'er all that had been great on earth."

But a resistance deriving its source from the deepest springs of the human heart has never ceased to oppose this wanton exercise of power; sedition may for a time have been quiet, and tranquillity have appeared on the surface of the land; let it not be imagined, however, that bayonets have chained the mind,—" *lo mormorito quetamente suona,*" and if Petrarch could arise from the dead to sing of Italian liberty, he would find the Venetian still gazing on the spoils of Constantinople, the Florentine on his knees within the holy precincts of Santa Croce, and the Roman musing among the edifices of the Forum. As hidden fires slumber beneath the volcanic rocks of the Apennines, so the armies of despotism crush the uprisings of a people cherishing an unquenchable desire to be free.

No one who has perused the foregoing pages will accuse me of contemning the fine arts; but there is a great difference between admiring the works of Raffaelle and Canova, and attaching to these works an influence highly beneficial to civilization. How many display a just sense of the beautiful, without feeling the want of what we in England now consider the necessaries of life! Not only does the workshop require much more mind and industry than the studio, but its benefits multiply themselves, and proportionably add to the material prosperity of a nation.

Hundreds of men in Italy are employed in providing "Madonnas" for the cottages of the peasants, little daubs of the Virgin Mary, the *penates* of a superstitious race; would it not conduce in a greater degree to the progress of the country, if they abandoned a pursuit so unrepro-

ductive, for the silk factory or the flax mill?
Vast fields of lint and hemp may be seen in most
parts of the Peninsula; but the labourers who for
ages ought to have been busy converting their
produce into garments, rope, and sail-cloth, have
been building palaces, cutting marble, and studying
paints; every one possesses a bad picture, but an
ill-furnished house,—a head of Dante, but scarcely
sufficient clothing to appear in open day; whilst
our middle classes enjoy the luxuries which reproductive industry places within their reach, the
admirer of æsthetic excellence south of the Alps
knows nothing of the comforts of home.

During the day he may lounge in the galleries
where Guido delights the eye, but in the evening
he returns to a dreary room in some old palazzo,
where, by the light of a glimmering candle, he
gropes his way to a tottering table and a crazy
bed; he may be able critically to examine the
masterpieces of Titian, but as a man of business
he is on a par with the Chippeway; an English
schoolboy has more acquaintance with real life,
and the backwoodsman on the Missouri can better
appreciate the useful arts. Manufactures, litera-

ture, and politics, are excluded from the thoughts of a people thus unnaturally engrossed with the beauties of design; and when any unforeseen occurrence disarranges the outward harmony of things, they rush to extremes, behave like irrational creatures, and rivet their chains.

The civilization of painting, statuary, architecture, and music has not reared the fabric of English greatness, nor raised in the western world one of the mightiest nations of the earth; we must look for its effects to Bavaria or Italy, where pictures employ thousands, and every villa has its rows of statues. In these as well as other countries government encourages, by every means in its power, a taste for the fine arts, knowing that those who devote themselves to this pursuit form the most obedient of unintelligent slaves. Whilst the inhabitants of Naples and Munich live more poorly than did the Saxons of the Heptarchy, the tradesmen of Liverpool and New York sit down in their well-furnished parlours, with their wives and children, to a meal consisting of articles known only to the noblesse of Italy. An English operative who reads Chambers's Journal and the

Mechanics' Magazine, is surely, notwithstanding his ignorance of artistic merit, a much more civilized being than the workman of Florence; however incapable of pronouncing on the beautiful, he is a more enlightened, a wiser, a more useful man.

It would be well for all countries whose people have been trained on the æsthetic principle, to devote a greater degree of attention to the ordinary arts of life, to reproductive industry, and the cultivation of a taste for what will benefit, leaving those who have leisure and money to discuss the humanising influences of music and statuary. Had we been producing frescoes instead of calicos, Glasgow might have been as Venice, and a foreigner occupying the throne of the Plantagenets. As long as human nature remains unchanged, the fine arts will have a prominent place among men; but to talk of their civilizing effects, shows an acquaintance neither with history, nor with the actual condition of Europe. It is no new idea that they have tended greatly to retard the civilization of Italy; and in every view of Italian affairs their influence, past and present, must not be lost sight of.

Let me now, however, direct the reader's attention more particularly to the political state of that Peninsula, the destinies of which seem at present entirely to depend upon the future history of Austria. Dr. Johnson somewhere remarks, that "the more contracted power is, the more easily it is destroyed,—a country governed by a despot is an inverted cone." No truer saying ever escaped the lips of a moralist; and it applies with double force to the bureaucracy of Vienna. Every one whom you meet in England fears "sad work on the continent soon;" notwithstanding all the precautions of tyranny, and the unfortunate effects of revolution, confidence has not been restored. And whither do we look for the outburst, or at least for the cabinet and dynasty which is least able to resist popular wrath? Assuredly to the banks of the Po and Danube, where Hungarians and Lombards writhe in their chains. In 1848, Metternich thought himself secure at Schönbrunn; and he was really so, compared with the present counsellors of the Archduchess Sophia, the virtual ruler of those various nations which the Congress of 1815 consigned to the tender mercies of the house of Hapsburg.

But whether political troubles arise or not, the storm has begun to gather in another quarter, a quarter from which it came before. "Nations," said Burke half a century ago, " are wading deeper and deeper into an ocean of boundless debt. Public debts, which at first were a security to government, by interesting many in the public tranquillity, are likely in their excess to become the means of their subversion. If governments provide for these debts by heavy impositions, they perish by becoming odious to the people. If they do not provide for them, they will be undone by the efforts of the most dangerous of all parties; I mean, an extensive, discontented monied interest, injured and not destroyed."* On this subject I appeal, not to Mr. Cobden, the advocates of peace, or the denouncers of foreign loans, but to every man who has studied the fluctuations of the Bourse at

* French Revolution, p. 219.

Vienna, or the efforts made by the cabinet to obtain money since the Hungarian war.*

If these obvious proofs of extreme need have not been noticed, let the candid mind weigh the sentiments expressed ten years ago by the most philosophical traveller who has yet described the dominions of Hapsburg beyond the Danube. " The Austrian exchequer," says Mr. Paget,† " it is well known, is and has been for centuries in a miserably low state; and there are no arts, except those of enlightened and honest administration, which have not been put in practice to improve it.. . . . The end of this government has been two national bankruptcies, the destruction of all commerce from without, and of all energy and enterprise within."

This account of things is sufficient to alarm every cautious capitalist; but how much have matters altered for the worse since 1842? A bloody, expensive war has occurred in Hungary;

* " It is indeed," says Sir Walter Scott, " on the subject of finance and taxation, that almost all revolutions among civilized nations have been found to hinge."—*Life of Napoleon*, chap. 83.

† " Hungary and Transylvania." By J. Paget, Esq. Vol. i. p. 409; vol. ii. p. 539.

an equally costly struggle has agitated Lombardy;
and at the present moment Austrian troops have to
be clothed, fed, and paid, to garrison both Holstein
and Tuscany. What sum it annually requires to
maintain this gigantic military establishment, the
war minister only knows; but every one may
safely put it down as something enormous.

Now, if it be true that armies are vast masses
of men, who ought to be engaged in productive
labour, grievously misemployed; if large sums of
money must be forthcoming to prevent mutiny;
and if pecuniary embarrassment stares Francis
Joseph in the face; what is to become of a dynasty
which, again to quote from Edmund Burke, "depends entirely upon the army," and has "indus-
triously destroyed all the opinions and prejudices,
and, as far as in it lay, all the instincts which
support government?" In Transylvania, every
official is sent to Coventry by the nobility; in
Hungary, wide-spread dissatisfaction prevails; the
Viennese sympathise with freedom; Russia tam-
pers with the Sclavonic races; and in Lombardy
you see only gaping cannon, ready at a moment's
notice to sweep the streets. It would require a

much more stable government than that of Austria
to retain permanent possession of the valley of the
Po. Its inhabitants have shown a restless, dis-
satisfied spirit during many ages : in the eleventh
century they burned Pavia to the ground; in the
twelfth they formed the league of Cremona against
Frederic Barbarossa, unawed by the capture and
destruction of Milan; and before that period closed
they had taught that haughty conqueror a lesson
which his successors would do well to keep in mind.

"By a certain class of statesmen," says Hallam,
"and by all men of harsh and violent disposition,
measures of conciliation, adherence to the spirit of
treaties, regard to ancient privileges or to those
rules of moral justice which are paramount to all
positive right, are always treated with derision.
Terror is their only specific, and the physical inability to rebel their only security for allegiance."*
These measures Barbarossa tried against the cities
of Lombardy; but he tried them in vain: at Leg-
nano they routed his formidable forces, and compelled him to conclude an armistice, which ended
in the peace of Constance and the liberties of Italy.

* Middle Ages, vol. i. p. 239.

By their disunion, the inhabitants did not preserve the prize thus nobly won; jealousy, faction, and civil hate, conspired again to open the Alpine passes to the Germans, and Milan became the possession of a foreign power. Thus Heaven punishes those who, wasteful of its gifts, blast by internal strife the prospects of their native land. But the spirit of the people has not yet been broken; they obey the myrmidons of bureaucracy, but they obey them with ill-dissembled reluctance; the uniform of Austria is an eyesore in town and country; they would rather trust the uncertain revolutions of the wheel of fortune than submit to the constant annoyances to which *espionnage* and martial law expose them; and whatever political events may happen in Europe, they will be ready to unfurl the standard of revolt. No one but the Eternal knows in what manner punishment will fall on the aggressor; but every consideration leads us to the conclusion, that a more precarious tenure does not exist than that by which a German army governs the north of Italy.

One of the most remarkable incidents in the late

war was the heroic defence of Venice. It reminded
us of her better days, when Dandolo, with his five
hundred ships, sailed to attack Byzantium; or
when John Palæologus passed under the Rialto to
visit the republic " strong in the sea." We north-
erns had the impression that every spark of Venetian bravery had been extinguished by the
tyranny of strangers and the influence of sloth;
but Manin opened our eyes to the gratifying fact,
that a love of freedom still prevails in the Queen
of the Adriatic; and that, if not destined to restore
her doge, she may yet occupy a prominent position
on the theatre of Italian politics.

Passing over Tuscany, which now, being gar-
risoned by Austrian soldiers, may be considered
part of Lombardy, we come to the Papal States,
the present political position of which must be
familiar to every educated Englishman. Sir Edward Bulwer Lytton has well said, that " a reforming Pope is a lucky accident; and dull indeed
must be the brain which believes in the possibility
of a long succession of reforming Popes, or which
can regard as other than precarious and unstable

the discordant combination of a constitutional government with an infallible head."* Most of the pontiffs have been raised to the chair when advanced in years; and, however benevolent in their disposition, have found themselves unable to resist the claims of relatives or the unworthy measures of official corruption.

It is not in the nature of things that the papal court should be otherwise than corrupt; in all ages the government has been nearly intolerable; and now, when other countries have made such giant strides, it remains more barbarous than ever. Agriculture is neglected, trade languishes, murders prevail, and robbers roam the mountains unawed by officer or priest. " Chi considera bene la legge evangelica," wrote Vettori in the sixteenth century, " vedrà i pontefici, ancora che tenghino il nome di vicario di Christo, haver indutto una nova religione, che non ve n'è altro di Christo che il nome ; il qual comanda la povertà e loro vogliono la richezza, comanda la humilta e loro vogliono la superbia, comanda la obedientia e loro vogliono comandar a ciascuno."

* Rienzi, preface, p. ix.

H 3

The occupation of Rome by the French, in order to keep out the Austrians, who already garrison Bologna, the second city in the states, can be more suitably discussed by the correspondents of newspapers than in these pages; its history is recent, and every one knows the circumstances. But the cardinals do not like their masters; and by all means in their power they are trying to disgust the government at Paris, in order to bring about the recal of those troops which stand in the way of German regiments. Devoted to Austrian interests, the priests hire ruffians to assault and murder General Gemeau's soldiers; and several of the latter expressed themselves to me heartily disgusted with their quarters. The people despise them, and the papal officers plot to annoy them; no wonder that both officers and men would rather serve their country in Algiers.

Let us turn from these distracted provinces to consider the state of matters at Naples,—that unhappy kingdom whose inhabitants owe Mr. Gladstone such a debt of gratitude for his manly *exposé* of an iniquitous government. To quote from his pamphlet would be unnecessary, for every one interested in the suppression of cruelty will read it, however few think of wasting time in perusing that reply, which, to our shame be it said, Ferdinand has found an Englishman unworthy enough to publish. Twenty thousand human beings in prison for political offences! A majority of the late Chamber of Deputies either exiled or in fetters! The executive power deliberately employing as spies the very dregs of society! Acquitted prisoners still in dungeons! Judges approving perjury, and browbeating witnesses! Poerio doomed to a death worse than beheading! Can we wonder that Mr. Gladstone calls such things "gigantic horrors, which prepare the way for a violent revolution" against a government, "itself the grand law-breaker and malefactor, the first in rank among oppressors, the deadly enemy of freedom and intelligence, the active fomenter and instigator of the vilest corruptions among the people?"

Further comment on this system of iniquity is scarcely necessary. The ruler who seeks to build his hopes of permanent power on the corruption of his people, who transgresses the limits of that "moral competence" inherent in the supreme authority, and thus makes rebellion no crime, is like a sailor walking the deck of his vessel, while combustion chars the bulkhead of the powder-magazine below. As soon as Paris or Vienna gives the signal, there will be nothing for the last of the Bourbons but exile or death.

There was another Ferdinand, who in the fifteenth century pursued at Naples a similar course —perfidious to his nobles, cruel to the middle class, calamity at length overtook him, and his posterity ceased to reign. But his modern namesake will not take warning, a judicial blindness seems to cover his eyes, and he continues a career of reckless tyranny, reminding me of that eloquent passage in Sheridan's invective against another branch of the same miserable race : " What but a superior abhorrence of that accursed system of despotic government which had so deformed and corrupted human nature as to make its subjects capable of such acts; a government that sets at nought the property, the liberty, and lives of the subjects; a government that deals in extortion, dungeons, and tortures; sets an example of depravity to the slaves it rules over:—and if a day of power comes

to the wretched populace, 'tis not to be wondered
at, however it is to be regretted, that they act
without those feelings of justice and humanity of
which the principles and the practice of their
governors have stripped them." How applicable
this description of the French Bourbons to their
cousins at Naples!

As long as corruption, cruelty, and despotism
desolate this unhappy country, we cannot expect
that Calabria will emerge from that barbarism
which for centuries has diverted from it the stream
of travellers, or renounce those superstitious practices which have never been uprooted among the
mountains since idolatry was destroyed. No one
requires to be told that Sicily has for many years
been ripe for rebellion; the massacre at Catania
and the bombardment of Messina sufficiently attest
that: but the traveller who has conversed with the
people on the mainland knows that they too show
as undoubted symptoms of a bloody outbreak, as
Vesuvius does of a near eruption, when smoke in
the form of a pine-tree fills with terror the inhabitants of the plain.

My remarks have hitherto been directed to the

dark side of the picture; but amidst this gloom there is hope, for freedom has not yet entirely deserted even Italy; one bright spot in the landscape relieves the wearied eye, and encourages expectations of a better future.

If the gift of prophecy has descended to modern times, in one instance at least it may be claimed by Sir Edward Bulwer Lytton. Many years ago, when Europe wore a very different aspect, he penned this remarkable sentence :—" The time must come when Sardinia will lead the van of Italian civilization, and take a proud place among the greater nations of Europe." That time has come—a people once torn asunder by intestine contentions, have united to follow the footsteps of England, by establishing and supporting a constitutional government, under which agriculture, manufactures, and the useful arts promise to flourish, as they have never yet done south of the Alpine ranges. Once Piedmont was the persecutor of the Waldenses, the incarnation of bigoted cruelty; now she has established liberty of worship, and a Protestant chapel is being erected at Turin : formerly her ministers approved of that prohibitory fiscal system from which commerce has suffered so much in the Mediterranean; but during the past year they have concluded a free-trade treaty with England, and prosperity has returned to Genoa to an extent even beyond the expectations of the most sanguine mind. What a change has this liberal policy produced within the last few years!

Not long ago the city of the Dorias seemed rapidly hastening, like Venice, to a premature decay; but of late that retrograde movement has been stopped; in 1849 I observed manifest symptoms of improvement, and in 1851 the appearance of the Porto Franco, or quarter of bonded warehouses, quite surprised me. One could scarcely move for the crowd of merchants, clerks, warehousemen, and porters, busily engaged among bale-goods and produce; the quays resembled those of Liverpool or New York, more than the deserted wharves of a declining land; and the business there transacted has so outgrown the capabilities of the harbour, that it is said government have determined to abandon the arsenal and dockyards to commercial purposes, and remove their establishment to La Spezzia.

Factories are likewise greatly increasing in number, especially along the Mediterranean coast; a railroad will soon connect Turin with its seaport; another has been fixed upon to the frontiers of Lombardy, and perhaps ere long we shall hear of Mr. Stephenson surveying the line of the Alps, with a view of tunnelling the mountains between the Rhone and the Val d'Aosta, or between Susa and the valley of the Isere.

It is really heart-cheering now to stand on the pier of Genoa, and contemplate the forest of masts within the mole,—to mix with the commercial men on the Bourse, or at the Porto Franco, and to see the vast amount of traffic on the road toward the lighthouse. I had heard of the rapid strides being made by Piedmont, but the reality surprised me. From Pietra Santa to Nice, from Spezzia to Geneva, marks of industry, energy, and progress on every side appear—admirable roads—well-cultivated fields—silk works—canvas manufactories—ship-building—railways—new villas; all bear witness to a rising people,—a people who must infallibly lead the civilization of Italy. They have no ruins amongst which to meditate, unless they be the

venerable walls of Genoese palaces; but the mantle
of England has fallen upon them, and when a
period of freedom has brought forth its proper
fruit, we may expect to see all that is good and
great in the Peninsula rallying round the throne of
Turin. How mysterious are the ways of that God
who has so ordered it that a country once the high-
place of ignorance, has become the very stronghold
and refuge of Italian patriotism! Watch well,
ye enemies of tyranny over the independence of
Sardinia, and the liberties of the Peninsula are
safe.

Unfortunately for Central and Southern Italy,
her people have no choice between despotism and
democracy. "What can we do?" asked some of them
whom I met while travelling, " we have no native
princes to lead us ; the Grand Duke of Tuscany is
an Austrian ; the Pope has made a league with our
oppressors ; the King of Naples is a tyrant of the
worst possible kind—one portion of the nobility
frowns on liberal principles—the other possesses
neither energy nor talent; we must trust to the
chapter of accidents, and, although no republicans
in theory, Mazzini is our man." I mourn this

lamentable want of royal leaders; but the fact no one can dispute.

In the fourteenth century Rienzi cherished a noble idea of uniting Italy in a great federal republic, of which Rome should be the head, and all the principal cities members. His messengers, bearing in their hands the white rods of embassy, traversed the Peninsula to explain this at that time visionary scheme, and everywhere the people on their knees asked Heaven to bless the undertaking. Italy for the Italians—union against the north—local administration, but mutual dependence —were the watch-words which more than three hundred years ago kindled a holy ardour in the breast of the last of the Tribunes.

Let us not too hastily decide that, after so many ages of a government under which municipal institutions have been nearly destroyed, republicanism cannot be adopted in the Peninsula, for history affords notable examples to render a contrary conclusion probable. No provinces enjoyed less liberty, or suffered more grievously from the bureaucratic principle than the Spanish colonies of America; yet every one of them has become a republic. Such has always been the tendency of the human mind—to rush from one extreme to another—when released from a despot's bonds to take refuge in the arms of democracy. But the evils of factious uncertainty will in every age be preferred to a degrading slavery; and wise men will consider it mere sophistry to oppose the cause of freedom, on account of "patriotism," as Dr. Johnson says, being "the last refuge of a scoundrel." Politicians of impracticable and visionary views will be found in every climate. It is a necessary evil attending popular movements, that those whose mouths never cease to sound the praises of liberty and charity may often be found at heart the most bitter tyrants; but none of these things affect the great principle involved; and where freedom has degenerated into licence, the careful student of history will find, that to the intolerant rulers must be ascribed the blame. My impression is, that republicanism, in one form or another, will establish itself on the ruins of despotic government in Italy.

We hear a great deal in certain quarters about the military strength of foreign powers, and the impossibility of disturbing that arrangement of states made by the Congress at Vienna; and had governments acted with wisdom, had they " arrested the advances of arrogance within the limits of safety,"* perhaps their position would have been secure : but it has not been so ; they have trampled on the rights of men, broken promises, annulled constitutions, bombarded towns, shot innocent victims, and given to their subjects a secret poison, which, intended to deaden their sensibilities, will first impart to them a delirious strength, and enable them to burst their bonds. I fear that before many years we shall see, what Macaulay justly denominates, " the most frightful of all spectacles—the strength of civilization without its mercy."† When oppression becomes intolerable, the fear of defeat no longer acts as a check on rebellious projects ; but despair begets an unnatural courage, the fiery cross flits from tribe to tribe, beacons blaze on the mountains, and the despot trembles on his throne.

It would be well if the three governments,

* Isaac Taylor's "Spiritual Despotism," p. 326.
† Essay on Warren Hastings, p. 9.

which now keep down Italy by armies, would take warning from the terrible though latent discontent of the people. Alfieri spoke to them a word in season when he exclaimed—

" Schiavi siam, ma schiavi ognor frementi;"

and there is not a man of education throughout the country, who, if he dared, would not tell a similar tale. Perhaps they trust to the want of leaders among the nobles, and the absence of patriotism among the national princes; but this affords no true ground of confidence, as in England, when Major Bridgenorth so prophetically addressed Peveril of the Peak—" The times demand righters and avengers, and there will be no want of them." *

John of Procida was a humble man, an insignificant, though devoted adherent of Manfred in his contest with Charles of Anjou for the Neapolitan sceptre; but when that struggle terminated disadvantageously, and his property reverted to the crown, he crossed over to Sicily ; travelling from town to town, spread disaffection against the

* Peveril of the Peak, vol. i. p. 180.

government of France; and so well did the people
conceal his projects, that no one, unacquainted with
the secret, knew of the impending blow till the
memorable eve of the *Sicilian Vespers*, when eight
thousand Gallic soldiers fell victims to popular
fury.*   The history of that awful night should be
carefully pondered by Ferdinand and Filangreri;
they now repose under shadow of Austrian pro-
tection, not heeding the murmurs of an oppressed
people, or the universal truth of Shakspeare's remark, "that the whirligig of time brings in its
revenges;" † but to me their conduct appears quite
inexplicable, unless on the principle, "Quem Deus
vult perdere, prius dementat."

There exists in Italy a feeling against the King
of Naples which makes one shudder; "the per-
jured," "the perfidious," "the assassin," such are the
terms used towards him even by those who talk of
the Grand Duke Leopold as a good-natured elderly
gentleman, unfit for his situation, and of Pio Nono
as the tool of more designing men; the latter they
would banish from the scene of their mis-govern-

* See Gibbon, vol. viii. Hallam's " Middle Ages," vol. i.
† Twelfth Night, Act v. Scene 1.

ment, the former they reserve to endure the punishment due to crime. It is a sad prospect for that lovely country; but who does not see the handwriting on the wall? I do not expect again to cross the Simplon until another Rienzi has awakened the echoes of the Forum, and the last of the Bourbons has shared the exile of his race.

The revolutionary troubles and the oppressions of the absolutist party, have combined to produce a most remarkable change in the sentiments of the Italian people regarding the Romish faith. In Lombardy, Tuscany, and especially in Rome itself, the established religion has received a shake which may well excite the alarm of its adherents; men cease to look up to the priests as oracles of wisdom, they cannot believe that God would commit to hands stained with the blood of their countrymen the sole keeping of his mysteries; finding church penalties so frequently used as a means of civil government, they have begun to treat them as of dubious authority; though still unacquainted with the Gospel, a few years more of despotism will, if we can trust present appearances, make them ripe for the reception of Protestant truth. In very few cases, it is true, do we see men actuated by opinions really evangelical; but let us not forget that similar beginnings ushered in the Reformation in Germany, and if south of the Alps another Luther should arise, who can foretell the consequences?

Since reaching home I find that other travellers in Italy, during the past summer, observed, like myself, the little interest apparently felt by the population in the holy festivals; few, in comparison with the multitudes of former years, joined the processions; the higher classes studiously absented themselves, the citizens gazed with indifference, many of them not even lifting their hats to the host; ladies exchanged jokes at the expense of burly fathers, and young men frowned on the pomp as a mere artifice of priestcraft. A small band of officers followed the monks and singing boys, while the soldiers bent their knees at the word of command, and thus the ceremony ended; the sacerdotal and military rulers retired to concert new measures of oppression, the people to meditate on the connexion between political tyranny and the religion of Rome. "I dare say," remarks a periodical writer, with reference to this state of things, "that a nation that shows so little respect for the holy services of their Church, is preparing, if not to leave, at least to reform her."

It is likewise well known to those acquainted with the country, that a considerable number of the parish priests,—men uninfluenced by the views of the hierarchy, sympathise both with national emancipation and ecclesiastical change; the demand for the Bible has filled the rulers, especially those of Tuscany, with alarm; scarcely a single Roman does not avow his leaning towards religious liberty; and in Sardinia a network of Protestant churches seems likely at no distant period to cover the land.

CHAPTER VIII.

NOTES ON THE POLITICAL INFLUENCE OF ROMAN CATHOLICISM.

THE LATITUDINARIAN PARTY IN ENGLAND—THEIR ALLIANCE WITH
THE ULTRAMONTANE ROMAN CATHOLICS—DIFFERENCE BETWEEN
THE AGENTS OF THE PAPACY IN BRITAIN AND THOSE ON THE
CONTINENT—AGGRESSIONS OF THE POPE IN THE SIXTEENTH CEN-
TURY—EFFECTS OF THE CATHOLIC EMANCIPATION ACT—PRO-
PHETIC WORDS OF SIR ROBERT PEEL — EXAMINATION OF THE
QUESTION REGARDING THE RIGHT OF THE ROMAN PONTIFF TO
APPOINT BISHOPS, TO CONTROL THE AFFAIRS OF NATIONAL
CHURCHES, AND TO EXERCISE TEMPORAL AUTHORITY — REAL
OBJECT OF THOSE REPRESENTED BY CARDINAL WISEMAN—INFLU-
ENCE OF POPERY ON MORALS AND LEARNING.

RECENT events in the history of our country have
introduced into the arena of political and ecclesiastical discussion a party, small in point of numbers, but influential inasmuch as they have in their
possession a portion of the public press, to whom,
without any breach of courtesy, may be applied
the epithet latitudinarian. Under the guise of moderation they hide a laxity of sentiment, which ren-

ders them dangerous counsellors in civil things, and apt to regard religious matters with a cold, sceptical indifference; their favourite saying is, Why attach so much stress to doctrinal varieties? let humanity, kindliness of disposition, and common sense be the tests of character: all their writings have as a motto that confused and ambiguous couplet—

> "For modes of faith let graceless zealots fight;—
> His can't be wrong whose life is in the right."

Two very different meanings may be gathered from these lines; but those who now-a-days continually quote them are at no pains to deny that, according to their opinion, a man may be a Christian, a Mahommedan, or a Buddhist, and yet a most respectable member of society. The difference between various sects who believe in the Bible, they consider as of no consequence whatever; the Roman Catholic and the Protestant—the Calvinist and the Universalist,—they look upon with equally favourable eyes; their superficial acquaintance with religious matters leads them, in the full assurance that oracular wisdom alone proceeds from their mouths, to pronounce evangelical

truth as a mere party symbol, without significance
or reality; and all sorts of opinions in regard to
the interpretation of Scripture appear to them alike
influential to promote individual virtue and social
happiness. Such people by their statements con-
tradict the remark of Cicero, that the true religion
could be but one, and that all others must be false;
they remind me of a sect which arose in Alex-
andria in the second century, who called themselve
Eclectics, because they adhered to no system in
particular, but chose a code for themselves, recog-
nising the Jew, the Pagan, the Grecian philosopher
and the Christian, as the same in the sight of
Deity. Loud in their professions of candour and
moderation, they were the most self-sufficient
theorists of the age; regarding Plato and Jesus
as virtually agreed, they understood neither the
philosophy of the one, nor the precepts of the
  ther; believing themselves free from prevalent
superstitions, they added a new kind of fanaticism
to the other corruptions of their time. Like them,
our modern latitudinarians affect the greatest zeal
for truth, while they take every opportunity to
attack its supporters; they ask credit for impar-

tiality, while straining every nerve, not to expose the *errors* of *all* systems, but to hold evangelical principles up to public reprobation; they proclaim a crusade against bigotry in general, but confine their efforts solely to the bigotry of zealous Protestant teachers;—liberality is their watchword, but the Gospel the real object of their dislike.*

The description which Burke gives of the school which had in his time risen into notice at Paris, applies with equal force to the indifferentism of the present day. " We hear these new teachers," says he, " continually boasting of their spirit of toleration. That those persons should tolerate all opinions who think none to be of estimation, is a matter of small merit. Equal neglect is not impartial kindness. The species of benevolence which arises from contempt is no true charity." † I have made these remarks on the conduct of a party whom every serious mind must look upon as the most dangerous enemies of Christianity, as a kind

* " The pillars of revelation are shaken by those men who preserve the name without the substance of religion, who indulge the licence without the temper of philosophy."—Gibbon's " Decline and Fall of the Roman Empire," chap. 1.
- † French Revolution, p. 213.

of introduction to a brief notice of the present position occupied by that venerable system of superstition, which seems, at least for the moment, to be the special object of their sympathy. It is a most singular circumstance, that the very men who arrogate to themselves the title of the only real advocates of civil and religious liberty, should be engaged heart and soul in defending the most grievous system of ecclesiastical tyranny which the world has ever seen. What a spectacle! The denouncers of intolerance forming a league of brotherhood with the legates of Rome! Behold the philosophers who devote their energies to exposing the priestly arts of Presbyterian pastors, eloquently describing the virtues of the Jesuits! The leading articles of certain organs of the so-called liberal party, during the late discussion on the measure introduced by Lord John Russell regarding Papal Aggression, were truly curiosities in literature, worthy of being preserved to illustrate the inconsistencies of the human mind. "This faction," wrote Isaac Taylor, several years ago, "now actually spread their shield over the enormities and follies of Romanism; and with sur-

prising eagerness step in to defend the good old
superstition against any new assailant. Thus the
very same Popery that was furiously run upon by
the sceptics of the last age, is as zealously be-
friended by the sceptics of this." ... "The summer
season of philosophic impiety is just at that time
when some degrading and gorgeous superstition
overawes the vulgar, decorates the frivolous hypo-
crisy of the opulent, and thickly shades from all
eyes the serious verities of religion." ... " English
unbelievers know better than to use any efforts for
demolishing the popular folly; on the contrary,
they give it the aid of their talents, and the mock
homage of their external reverence." *

No apology need be offered to the reader for
here introducing this remarkable passage; it describes the phenomenon, and assigns its cause. If
any real adherent to Protestantism continues, in
neglect of the warning here given, to seek the alliance of a party, indifferent to scriptural truth,
and pledged to defend a monstrous system of oppression, he deserves to suffer the penalties which,
sooner or later, Ultramontane Romanism hopes

* Spiritual Despotism, pp. 16, 18.

to inflict on its dupes. Shunning the bugbear of intolerance amongst those of his own creed, he will assuredly find that none can persecute so bitterly as the Jesuit and the infidel.

One of the most successful of the artifices, by means of which this "Holy Alliance" have been lately attempting to deceive the British public, is to enlarge upon the intelligence, worth, and zeal of the Roman Catholics in our own land; while they keep in the background the state of those continental countries where Popery prevails. The Italian hides his indifference under a mantle of ceremony, the Frenchman trifles with the rites of the Church as with a legionary decoration or a pole of liberty; the earnest Anglo-Saxon alone gives dignity even to the abuses of priestcraft. This the agents of Rome well know, and they seem to have imparted their knowledge most assiduously to their quondam allies; but to judge of the system from its manifestations in England would lead us to a most fallacious conclusion; we do not want to know the appearance of Popery surrounded by and battling with Protestantism, but its appearance in countries where its development has not been checked by counteracting causes; we want to see it exposed to open day, not wearing a mask, which hides every hateful feature from the inquiring gaze.

Those who have been in Madrid, Lisbon, Munich, Naples, Lima and Rio de Janeiro, can testify how different the ignorant licentious priests of these cities are from the English emissaries of Rome. The men who, in London, profess extraordinary liberality, who in Dublin welcome with open arms a Protestant ally, who in Edinburgh deplore the bigotry of Presbyterianism, are the same men who in Florence imprison readers of the Bible, who in Rome deny Britons liberty to worship, who in Spain refuse Protestants Christian burial, who in Lombardy prohibit the circulation of the word of God, who in Naples reward the supporters of religious freedom with the rack or the dungeon. And these are the parties whom we Britons are *persecuting* because we refuse to sanction the establishment of an *imperium in imperio;* because we seek to protect the more loyal of our Roman Catholic countrymen from the operation of an iniquitous canon law; because we check at the beginning the aggressions of a power which has already absolved

subjects from their allegiance, and may do so again.
This is not the first encroachment of Roman
tyranny on the liberties of England.

When swarms of Jesuits arrived on our shores
during the reign of Elizabeth, her officers demanded
an explicit answer to the question :—" Do you consider the anathema of Pius V. against your Queen
lawful and binding?" but no reply could be ex-
torted from these crafty men, more satisfactory
than that they wished to " render unto Cæsar the
things that were Cæsar's, and unto God the things
that were God's;" this subterfuge the judges inter-
preted as a confession of guilt, and they treated the
emissaries as rebels, sent by a haughty Pontiff to
plot against the crown. Again, in the sixteenth
century, William Allen, leading the Ultramontane
party in England, solemnly declared :—" Si reges
Deo et Dei populo fidem datam fregerint, vicissim
populo non solum permittitur, sed etiam ab eo pas-
tore, ipse quoque fidem datam tali principi non
servet!" This revolutionary doctrine, Cardinal
Bellarmine, in a well-digested work,* not only
sanctioned, but defended at great length; at that

* De Conciliorum Auctoritate.

time no one looked upon it as unusual; it was recognised as natural to Popery, and dealt with accordingly. Fifty years later, Urban VIII. demanded that Roman Catholic churches should be built at the public expense in every English county;* but there were then neither Aberdeens nor Grahams, so the proposal was received, as it ought to have been, with indignation and contempt. Were it renewed in 1852, we might see it warmly applauded by a few statesmen coquetting with Ireland, and a literary phalanx, who wage bitter war against evangelical truth. These parties seem unable to distinguish between liberality and latitudinarianism, between giving men their civil rights and picking the pockets of others to pay for their ceremonies; they would not only bestow upon Roman Catholics the franchise, but patronise, cherish, and pamper them by every means in their power. Against this most fatal policy, it appears to me that all Protestants and patriots should cordially unite; for, if persevered in, it will assuredly subvert the liberties of our land.

Dr. Chalmers in his later years, spoke of Catholic

* Ranke's "History of the Popes," vol. ii. p. 269.

Emancipation as a " historical blunder;" not that he regretted the passing of that righteous measure, or doubted its political justice; but that he, in common with many other great and good men amongst its advocates, felt that the hopes founded on it respecting the feelings of the Irish masses, had not been realized.   It was to restore harmony to our empire, to heal the wounds inflicted by party strife, to destroy the influence of unprincipled agitators, to remove the cause of discontent, to make Connemara a garden of roses, and Tipperary the abode of peace.   How have these expectations been disappointed! Does not history and experience warn us, after political rights have been granted, to make no covenant with Rome?   To attempt by favours and bribery to make loyal subjects of men ruled by the Vatican, is a task too herculean even for the statesmen of England.   Far be it from me to include in this condemnation of duplicity and ingratitude all the Catholics of our country; my remarks refer only to the party led in Ireland by John of Tuam, and across the Channel by the Bishop of Melipotamus, legate of the Holy See. This faction must be ruled with firmness, not coaxed to behave; watched as subjects of a foreign power, not salaried as officers of the British crown; they have got justice, now they desire domination; they sit in Parliament, now they wish to bend cabinets to their ambitious ends; and if before them we Protestants quail, we may expect to see the Privy Council of England the catspaw of Austria and creature of the Pope.

It is now more than twenty years ago since Sir Robert, then Mr. Peel, whose loss we so much deplore, when introducing the Catholic Emancipation Bill into the House of Commons, used these remarkable, almost prophetic words:—" I trust by the means now proposed, that the moral storm may be lulled into calm, that the waters of strife may subside, and the elements of discord be stilled and composed. *But if these expectations be disappointed, if, unhappily, civil strife and contentions shall still take place, if the differences which exist between us do not arise out of artificial distinctions and unequal privileges, but if there be something in the character of the Roman Catholic religion, a something not to be contented with a participation of equal privileges, or anything short of superiority,* still I shall be content to make the trial." The great statesman seemed even then to fear in the midst of hope, and to see, through the mists of party warfare, the shadows of events which were to come; if Providence had spared him to witness the renewal of the storm, we cannot doubt on which side his powerful voice would have been heard.

During the recent discussions in England regarding the papal bull, it has been frequently asserted, and as frequently denied, that the appointment of bishops and organization of dioceses by the Pope were necessary for the due government of the Church; that the proclamation decreeing them was no foreign encroachment, but an ecclesiastical act, recognised as regular by every true son of the Romish faith.

Let us go back to history, and examine this knotty question with care; for upon the answer to it depends in some measure the solution of the whole matter at issue. If the Pope has the sole right of nominating dignitaries and managing Church temporalities throughout the Catholic world, then his acts, in those respects, must be considered as incidental to the system; if not, then it becomes the duty of civil governments to protect their subjects against his attacks, looking upon him as a foreign potentate rather than as an ecclesiastical ruler, as the high-priest of despotism rather than as the head of the Church. Because the majority of a nation are Protestant, it does not follow that the government are not bound to see that no one interferes with the ecclesiastical liberties of the Roman Catholic portion of the community; if priestly influence persuade many of the latter to give up their rights, that is no reason why the remainder should be compelled to conform. But if, on the contrary, no aggression has been attempted; if nothing unusual or inconsistent with ecclesiastical practice has been proclaimed, it becomes a religious question, interesting only to members of a particular Church, with which we as citizens have nothing whatever to do.*

The careful student, who wishes to understand the history and extent of the power of the popes, will find that, about the end of the eighth century,

---

* On this subject the reader will find important information in Antonio de Dominis' work, "De Republica Christianâ;" in which he demonstrates the inadmissibility of the Pope's claim to destroy the independence of Christian bishops.

there appeared a collection of canons, purporting to be rescripts or decrees of the early bishops of Rome, in which power was given to the Pontiff to forbid national councils, to appoint, correct, and remove bishops, to erect new sees, and to translate dignitaries from one see to another.* These decretals, which every one regarded as a palpable imposture, and the Gallican Church from the beginning treated with scorn, were acted upon by Alexander II., whom we all know was the mere tool of Hildebrand; and Gregory VII. boldly announced his determination not to recognise national synods, by citing all the provincial bishops to Rome.† But even he, the great champion of papal rights, did not dare to claim the nomination of ecclesiastical dignitaries in Germany; he referred the choice to the chapters, and merely insisted upon his right to confirm the validity of the election.‡

When, in the twelfth century, the popes procured from the emperors a renunciation of their rights of investiture, these rights devolved not on the Roman

* Hallam's "Middle Ages," vol. i. p. 524.
† Ibid. vol. i. p. 548.
‡ Ranke's "History of the Popes," vol. i. p. 21.

see, but on the chapters of cathedral churches.* The same compromise was then effected in England; but in Spain † the monarch retained that power which his fellow-sovereigns had been forced to yield up to ecclesiastics. But not long afterwards, first as a favour, then as a right, the pontiffs gradually began to fill up vacant benefices with their own nominees; and in 1266, Clement IV. published a bull, asserting it to be the absolute prerogative of the successors of St. Peter to dispose of all preferments.‡

Only thirty years previously, however, the famous Grosseteste had been elected to the see of Lincoln by the dean and chapter,§ and from that time to his death he ceased not to denounce the ambition of Rome. " He would often with indignation," says the historian, " cast the papal bulls out of his hands, and absolutely refuse to comply with them." Innocent peremptorily ordered him to admit an Italian to a rich benefice: Grosseteste

* Hallam's " Middle Ages," vol. i. p. 546.

† In that country, Julianus, now a canonized saint, freely censured Pope Benedict II. for interfering with the action of the national synods.—See Schlegel's Note to Mosheim, Cent. VII.

‡ Hallam's " Middle Ages," vol. ii. p. 13.

§ Milner's " Church History," Century XIII. chap. vii.

firmly refused to obey, and was suspended; but the suspension was not recognised as lawful, and he continued to perform every function of his office in defiance of the papal mandates.

In the year 1281 a council was held in Lambeth, to regulate the affairs of the Church; and so far from looking upon as necessary those acts which in 1851 some people tell us have from time immemorial been regarded as undoubtedly belonging to the Holy See, the ecclesiastics there assembled gave the cup to the laity, and introduced other reforms without any sanction from Rome. Early in the next century Edward III. secured the rights of patrons of livings against papal usurpation, and outlawed those who dared to appeal to Rome.[*]

In 1414 was held the celebrated Council of Constance, which declared the Pope subject to councils, thereby establishing the liberties of the Gallican Church, and setting bounds to the claims of the pontiffs.[†] Martin V., in 1448, restored episcopal elections to the chapters; and Charles VII. of France soon afterwards, by the Pragmatic Sanction of Bourges—the Magna Charta of the French

[*] Milner's "Church History," Century XIV. chap. i.
[†] Hallam's "Middle Ages," vol. ii. p. 43.

Church—deprived the Holy See of its usurped privileges.* Under Leo X. several princes of Germany obtained a restitution of the rights of investiture;† and with him Francis I. concluded a concordat, "wherein," says the historian, "the principle for which Gregory VII. had moved the whole world was with little difficulty resigned."

When we come down to later times, we find still constant protests against the usurpations of Rome. On the 17th of April, 1606, Paul V. pronounced sentence of excommunication on the doge, senate, and government of Venice, and interdicted the clergy of the territory from performing their sacred duties, under pain of rigorous punishments from God and man. The offence had been a resistance of claims founded on the very decretals mentioned at the beginning of this statement; but instead of overawing the republicans, this strong measure caused a schism in the Church. The Pope was amazed, and at length compelled to withdraw his awful edict.‡

Fifty years afterwards, the estates of the German

---

* Hallam's "Middle Ages," vol. ii. pp. 51, 52.

† Ranke's "Popes," vol. i. p. 29.

‡ Ibid. vol. ii. pp. 110, 130.

empire remonstrated against Roman interference with ecclesiastical elections;* and in 1682, the Gallican bishops passed three most important resolutions, the first excluding Rome from interfering with the temporal concerns of kings, the second acknowledging a general council to be superior to the pope, the third asserting the rights of the national Church, the fourth denying the infallibility of papal decisions, unless confirmed by a council.†

Thus we see that what certain parties now declare essential to the due government of the Romish Church has been regarded in all ages and in all countries as an *encroachment* of the Papal See on national liberties; that general councils have declared it an *innovation;* and that against it France, England,‡ and Germany have not ceased to *protest* and *complain.* Sometimes the pontiff contrived to exercise the disputed power; but it never remained long in his hands, and more than once he has been obliged to renounce his right to

* Ranke's "Popes," vol. ii. p. 412.
† Milner's "Church History," Century XVII. chap. ii.
‡ On the practice of the Catholic Church in England, see Murdock's Notes on Mosheim, Century II. part i. chap. 1.

possess it. This power Pius IX. now claims, through Cardinal Wiseman, supported by the majority of the Irish dignitaries. A few bold English Catholics are yet found to renew the protests of Grosseteste against Papal usurpation; but when we attempt to protect their rights and money, a small political party, and a more numerous latitudinarian faction, step forward to accuse us of breaking the great principles of religious liberty. The Pope, the Puseyites, and the sceptical press, unite to defend ecclesiastical freedom, to fight the battles of Hildebrand in the Parliament of England. What a strange confederacy! Could Gregory VII. arise from his tomb, what would he think of his new associates? But the heart of the British people is yet sound, and every unbiassed observer of past events knows well that the bull brought by Cardinal Wiseman was a political, not a religious measure, the act of an Austrian camarilla, not of the head of the Church.

The great object of the continental despots, both civil and ecclesiastical, is to create dissension in England, and thereby to weaken England's power, to provide difficulties for her statesmen in Ireland, in order to prevent them attending to the affairs of countries robbed by priestcraft and commanded by cannon. The combination appears at present strong; but defeat infallibly awaits it, for energies too powerful now oppose the ambition of a hierarchy; the strongest sympathies of the human soul rise against its domination; and those who knew the Rome of the Gregories will pity the puny efforts of Pio Nono, kept prisoner on his pontifical throne by the bayonets of France.

It is consoling for us to know, that amongst our Roman Catholic fellow-subjects there are men like the nobles of Bohemia, who, though opponents of John Huss, joined the banner of a national army, raised to oppose the forces sent by the Pope to destroy the Reformers. By adopting firm measures, we shall no doubt have, at least for a time, to expect a determined opposition on behalf of the Irish Catholics; but as the Glover said, in the "Fair Maid of Perth,"* "Never was there an extremity so pinching, but what a wise man might find counsel, if he was daring enough to act upon

* Vol. ii. p. 152.

it. This has never been the land or the people over whom priests could rule in the name of Rome, without their usurpation being controlled."

It will be readily admitted, that the people of this country have no right to interfere with purely ecclesiastical affairs pertaining to the government of the Roman Catholic Church; at the same time the careful student of history will not fail to observe, that there are matters in relation to the policy of that system, which so momentously affect the best interests of civil society, that no wise legislature should overlook them. Even the excesses of other sects may occasionally require state interference; if the practices of fanatical Mormons were in Britain, as in America, to outrage the customs of the nation, and violate universally acknowledged moral laws, the magistrate would be called upon to suppress them; much more, then, must we be on our guard against the *political* projects of a Church which has excommunicated kings, absolved subjects from their allegiance, sanctioned the *Institutes* of Ignatius Loyola, and openly avowed itself possessed of temporal authority.

In all ages there have been two distinct parties in the society which acknowledges the Roman Pontiff as its spiritual head,—a national party, believing the doctrines but resisting the aggressions of the Papacy,—an Ultramontane party, thirsting for boundless power, and making little or no difference between ecclesiastical and civil things: the former, however dangerous, even politically, not to say in a religious point of view, their doctrines may be, have always conducted themselves as good citizens; the latter must be watched as foreign spies, who may have a dispensation to depart from truth, and, while apparently the most zealous friends of order, to attempt the subversion of a nation's liberties.

It is likewise very necessary in this liberal age to keep our eyes open to the effects which Popery has, in nearly every instance, produced abroad: as patriots we have a right, not only to study, but to legislate with reference to them, though debarred from any interference in ecclesiastical matters. If we observe that immorality and crime have ever kept pace with the advances of a religious system; if we see the population of those

countries, where its influence is predominant and
its rites most rigorously observed, more debauched
and polluted than their neighbours, surely guided
by an instinct of self-preservation, we cannot be
found fault with for adopting precautionary
measures. However modified to suit different
states of society, or diverse mental constitutions,
there are some of the Roman Catholic doctrines
which, *per se*, must be deemed inconsistent with
freedom of conscience and rational liberty. Their
effect on learning and the arts need not for a
moment be doubted; a vast majority of great
scholars, profound mathematicians, acute meta-
physicians, and clever mechanists, have been found
in the ranks of Protestantism; and what is more
striking still, few, if any, among the Roman
Catholic literati of the last two or three centuries,
have really believed the doctrines which they
professed. To borrow the expressions of an
annalist,* himself devoted to the Papacy, the tenth
century, when Popery had reached its zenith,
" was an iron age, barren of all goodness; a leaden

* Baronius.

age, abounding in all wickedness; and a dark age, remarkable above all others for the scarcity of writers and men of learning." In fact, the influence of Roman Catholicism has been sensibly declining ever since the revival of letters in Europe; and though the system may change its hues like the chameleon to meet new emergencies, every such alteration betrays weakness and a departure from fundamental laws. If the Papacy is to recover its lost vigour, we must bid farewell to political liberty, to the cheap printing-press, to the steam-engine, the telegraph, and power-loom; we must ignore all modern inventions, and return contented to mediæval night.

Having already, while treating of Spain, adverted to the remarkable difference between Protestant and Roman Catholic countries, I need not again invite the reader's attention to this most instructive subject;* but conclude these remarks on the *effects* of Popery, by quoting the eloquent words of Mr. Macaulay, in his review of Ranke's History of the Popes: "The experience of twelve

* See Macaulay's "History of England," vol. i. p. 49.

hundred eventful years, the ingenuity and patient care of forty generations of statesmen, have improved that polity to such perfection, that amongst the contrivances which have been devised for deceiving and oppressing mankind it occupies the highest place."

CHAPTER IX.

NOTES ON THE POLITICAL INFLUENCE OF ROMAN CATHOLICISM—(*continuea*).

PROFESSED LIBERALITY OF PAPAL AGENTS—BEARINGS OF THEIR LEADING DOCTRINES ON CIVIL SOCIETY—THE CRUSADES—ASCETICISM —MARIOLATRY—PILGRIMAGES — PRETENDED 'MIRACLES— OBSERVATIONS ON THE HISTORY AND INFLUENCE OF AURICULAR CONFESSION—SOME EFFECTS PRODUCED BY THE CELIBACY OF THE CLERGY — MONASTERIES AND CONVENTS IN ENGLAND— "PERSECUTION A NECESSARY ELEMENT OF THE ROMISH CHURCH THEORY"—THE INQUISITION—THE CONFLICTS IN FRANCE—THE HUGUONOTS—CLOSING REMARKS.

IT has become fashionable of late in certain circles, to talk of Roman Catholicism as changed, and to laugh at the fears of those who think, that, however it may have adapted itself to altered circumstances, the system has undergone no real improvement since Hildebrand issued his mandates, and Ignatius filled the dungeons of the Inquisition.

The Latitudinarian party tell us that we Protestants are much more bigoted than the Romanists, who in England appear under the guise of extraordinary liberality; but let us raise the mask, and attentively consider the lessons of history, and we shall find that Popery has in all ages set up an Acesian ladder, by which its own adherents, and they alone, should ascend to heaven. To argue this point is really wasting words; every schoolboy knows that exclusiveness has characterised, and must characterise, the Papacy wherever found; and as if to throw ridicule on the statements of the Holy Alliance, Pio Nono declared in his Encyclical Letter, published in 1848, "Unionem cum catholica ecclesia, extra quam nulla est salus."

It will be profitable here briefly to consider some of those matters connected with Roman Catholicism which have an evident bearing on civil society, and therefore are legitimate subjects for legislative enactment. The doctrine of justification by works and the belief in miracles, both inherent in Popery, have produced various kinds of striking fanaticism, and these epidemical phrensies have done infinite injury to the finest countries in Europe. I need not in illustration of this statement refer to the Crusades, or attempt to describe the cruelty, licentiousness, and ignorance of those soldiers who waged war for the Holy Sepulchre with the Saracens, whose rapine became so fearful, that even Christians fled in terror before them; * nor would it be desirable at any length to examine the history of that asceticism which filled with half-savage men the Syrian and Libyan deserts. The incidents of the former are familiar to us as household words; and most men of education will recollect the account which has been handed down of the naked hermits or βόσκοι, who grazed like cattle on the fields of Mesopotamia, and dwelt with wild animals in the caves of Thebais; nor will Simeon Stylites be forgotten, the young Syrian who resisted the heat of thirty summers on the top of a column apart from the habitations of men. Even those who read only novels know something of this strange species of enthusiasm, for never was ascetic described in language so magnificent as that used by Sir Walter Scott in the " Talisman." " I am Theodorick of

* See Gibbon's "Decline and Fall of the Roman Empire,' vol. vii. p. 355.

Engaddi; I am the torch-brand of the desert; I am the flail of the infidels! The lion and the leopard shall be my comrades, and draw nigh to my cell for shelter; neither shall the goat be afraid of their fangs: I am the torch and the lantern. Kyrie Eleison." *

Let the story of Jesuitism be traced from its rudiments to the present time; from Loyola, on the steps of the Church of St. Dominic beholding the Trinity in Unity, to his disciples, propagating by means altogether unworthy the creed of Catholicism to the ends of the earth. But for examples of fanaticism, we do not require to search the records of mediæval times; in the nineteenth century it still prevails under the wings of the Papacy. Mr. Curzon, in his delightful work,* tells us, that "at the exhibition of the sacred fire in the church of the Holy Sepulchre at Jerusalem, the dead were lying in heaps, even upon the stone of unction; and that he saw four hundred wretched people, dead and living, heaped promiscuously one upon another, in some places above five feet high."

* Talisman, p. 58.
† Visit to the Monasteries of the Levant, p. 205.

In how many countries, likewise, has the religion of Jesus degenerated into a mere enthusiastic adoration of the Virgin Mary! This kind of worship has been patronised of late to a greater extent than ever by the priests of Italy; and the stranger who visits Milan, will find in one of the churches there an altar-piece, representing two ladders reaching from earth to heaven, with Christ at the top of one, and Mary at the head of the other : by the former, no one succeeds in ascending; by the latter, all are joyfully climbing to Paradise. No wonder that Nestorius protested against the title of Mother of God, and that when the Portuguese presented the image of the Virgin to the disciples of St. Thomas in India, they indignantly exclaimed, "We are Christians, not idolaters."* Mariolatry is a species of fanaticism, subversive of true religion, and most inimical to the progress of society; and it, as well as the other evils just mentioned, must be closely watched by an enlightened government. There is one practice encouraged, and even commanded by the Roman Catholic Church, productive of so much

* See Gibbon's "Decline and Fall of the Roman Empire," vol. vi. p. 72.

misery and suffering, that no Protestant country could tolerate it. It may be doubted if any superstition prevalent amongst the heathen has caused such destruction of human life as the pilgrimages of peaceable nations. Some writers calculate that more people have fallen victims to this delusion on their journeys to Benares, Mecca and Loretto, than have been killed by the sword and famine during the wars of 1,800 years. Religious pilgrimages have in all ages proved the most fatal; no path shows so many graves as that which leads to a holy sepulchre. Those who follow it do not take precautions, they provide not means to ensure their safety; but, impelled by a phrensy which sees no dangers, they rush with headlong enthusiasm into the very jaws of death. And then what manifold evils of another kind have attended these journeys! Their history reveals crimes of the deepest dye, the most unblushing licentiousness, the very perfection of rapine and cruelty. While Christianity scatters mankind over the world, to enjoy in all places the presence of God, superstition attracts towards some desert spot a crowd of ignorant immoral men, who spread desolation around their path, and leave their bones to whiten by an anchoret's tomb. The Turks have a maxim, which carries with it "the sting of truth:" "If your friend has made the pilgrimage once, distrust him; if he has made the pilgrimage twice, cut him dead."* This then appears to me a fit subject for legislation, though connected with the doctrines of a particular church.

It is strange that men of education should see anything to admire in the ceremonies of the Papacy; they have always struck me as most humiliating to rational beings; and it need scarcely form a matter of surprise, that a people accustomed to reverence them should be left far behind in the march of civilization. Even in the fourth and fifth centuries, the rites of Christianity had been so much altered, that had Tertullian beheld the incense, the flowers, the waxen tapers, the images, and fictitious relics, he would not have recognised the religion which he preached with so much power in the public places of Carthage. When, too, we read of emperors presenting to emperors portions of the true cross, the baby-linen of the Son of God,

* See "Eothen," p. 166.

the lance, the sponge, and the chain of his passion, the rod of Moses, and part of the skull of John the Baptist,* we scarcely know whether the authors of the imposture most deserve punishment, or their victims pity.

"If the Christian Apostles, St. Peter and St. Paul, could," says Gibbon, "return to the Vatican, they might possibly inquire the name of the Deity who is worshipped with such mysterious rites in that magnificent temple." Some minds are so constituted that no superstition appears to them too absurd or incredible; such people may be conscientious believers in priestly fabrications, and yet loyal subjects; but it will become a well-ordered state closely to watch the crafty deceivers: men who depart from truth in religion will not hesitate also to be unscrupulous in politics.

There are two practices distinguishing the Roman Catholic Church which, in my opinion, of themselves justify interference on the part of Government,—not to prevent their adoption, but to restrain their excesses; viz. auricular confession, and the celibacy of the clergy. These may be

* Gibbon's "Decline and Fall of the Roman Empire," vol. vii. p. 534.

ecclesiastical ordinances, but they are also political engines; the Pope may decree their establishment, but the magistrate must control them. In popish countries they produce unmixed and unchecked evils. If we cannot, consistently with religious liberty, destroy the corrupting influence, we can and ought to punish those who, for wicked ends, exercise their ghostly power. The priest who at the confessional advises an Irishman to shoot the bailiff, is to all intents and purposes a murderer, and ought, without mercy, to suffer the penalty of his crimes. If some of those who from the altar denounced particular individuals had been summarily led to punishment, we should have seen life and property safer in counties whose state reflects the deepest disgrace on men professing to be Christians.*

To trace the history and effects of auricular confession would be an interesting though painful task;† we first hear of it in Upper Egypt, from whence the Greeks introduced it as a condition of admission into the mysteries of Eleusis. The

* See Major Edwardes' "Year on the Punjaub Frontier," vol. i. p. 247, for an eloquent passage on this subject.
† See Count de Lasteyrie's "History of Auricular Confession."

Talmud enjoins it; the Siamese practised it before the introduction of Christianity; the Buddhists regard it as a sacred institution; Zoroaster harangued his disciples in its defence; and when Pizarro crossed the Andes, he found it among the Indians of Peru. From these heathen nations the first corrupters of Divine truth learned it; and it has since become an ordinance of the Eastern as well as the Western Church. The Greeks, however, forbid the priests to question the penitent; and the latter is not bound to reveal everything, but merely such offences as require ministerial advice.

Bishop Fenelon tells us that he sought diligently throughout the biography of the orthodox fathers, examined the minutest details of their lives and religious practices, and found not one single word about this practice; many historians have done the same, and with like success; we may therefore conclude that it formed no part of Christianity in the primitive ages, but was a corruption derived by crafty men from a heathen source.

It is related of Cardinal Ximenes, that when he retreated from the theatre of public affairs to enjoy the quiet of a Franciscan monk, he found himself absorbed in a vortex of worldly passions and interests, because obliged to listen to the confessions of the multitudes whom his fame attracted to the monastery.* This is but a small part of the evil caused by the narration of various sins to the priestly adviser. The penitent may be in no respect improved by the unblushing recital of dishonourable faults; but what must be the effect on the mind of the confessor, the receptacle of all the licentious tales which erring men and women have to tell him?

. The Church enjoins not only a GENERAL account of every sin, but a DETAILED and CIRCUMSTANTIAL narration of it in all its particulars. " Colligitur præterea," says the Council of Trent, " etiam eas circumstantias in confessione explicandas esse, quæ speciem peccati mutant." It is frightful to contemplate the impurity which day by day passes through the minds of Romish priests; and after reading the disclosures made by some of them in books revealing the secrets of the confessional, we can scarcely wonder at the general immorality

* See Prescott's " History of Ferdinand and Isabella," vol. ii. p. 349.

where Popery exercises a predominant influence. Placed in a position which Providence never designed that men should occupy, it is not surprising that the priests of the Romish faith should in many countries have thrown off all restraints of discipline and moral law.

Those conversant with the history of the Reformation will remember a little book written by Luther in the castle of Wartburg, concerning the abuses of private confessions, wherein he graphically describes the sinful practices of the monks—insinuating themselves into the houses of the opulent, to gain an influence over their minds; threatening them, on their death-beds, with the direst penalties, if they did not give the Church a prominent position in their wills; and destroying the peace of families by corrupting the minds of the young. How many estates in Christendom have been wrested from the rightful heirs by means of monkish absolutions *in articulo mortis!* How seared must have been the consciences of those ecclesiastics who in the Council of the Lateran sanctioned this crying evil!

When we turn from the seductions and robberies

resulting from auricular confession, to its political effects,* we can well understand the remark of Voltaire, that priestly advisers have been the source of most of the violent measures pursued by princes of the Catholic faith. Instances of this will readily occur to the minds of all conversant with European history. In the course of several journeys in various parts of Europe, I have met zealous Roman Catholics who regarded this institution with such horror, that they had absolutely prohibited their wives and daughters from sanctioning it by their presence: and no wonder, for at this very moment there live in Italy women who, under priestly direction, denounced their husbands to the Holy Office; and, to gratify monkish passions, sacrificed the dearest sympathies of life.

In the annals of heathen idolatry there are no crimes more horrible than those which may, without difficulty, be traced in a direct line to the hateful practice of auricular confession. It makes hypocrites and profligates of religious teachers, gives

---

* When the premises of the Inquisition were broken open in Rome in 1848, documents were found showing that Government had systematically made use of sacramental confession as a political engine.

one class an undue influence over society, sows dissension in families, corrupts pure minds, diverts inheritances from the natural channel, encourages intrigue, and paves the way for the political priest to propagate revolutionary principles. The law cannot prevent its secret practice, but it can visit upon those who have been convicted of applying it to improper purposes the severest penalties on the statute-book. A few such instances of well-merited punishment would, more effectually than bribes and royal gifts, check the usurpations of Rome.

The grievous effects produced by the celibacy of the clergy show themselves less frequently in civil affairs; yet they deserve a brief consideration here. This ordinance was established by the Council of Placentia in 1095,* but in all ages Roman Catholics have been found to condemn it; and even Pius II. before he became Pope pleaded earnestly for its reversal. † "Certainly," remarks Lord Bacon, "a wife and children are a kind of discipline to humanity." There is much truth in this saying. Every one has observed the more

---

* Milner's "Church History," Century XI. chap. i.
† Mosheim's "Church History," Century X.

obvious evils connected with the celibacy of the priesthood, the profligacy, licentiousness, and infidelity which it has caused; but a more attentive examination of mental history will show us disadvantages of another kind. Shut out from the happier influences to which laymen are accessible, the priest becomes an unnatural being; he indulges excited feelings, opinions not founded on fact, but formed by a morbid brain; fanaticism gradually acquires dominion over him, and he, perhaps a humane man before his initiation, wields with no light hand the sword of persecution. No wife generates feelings of tenderness in his mind, no children relieve the ruggedness of life; he mopes in solitude, a gloomy ascetic—rushes into dissipation, to supply a want which nature dictates—or presides in the Inquisition, to gratify a fanatical excitement, the disease of minds uninfluenced by means which God has appointed for the due government of man.

It has often been remarked in connexion with the lunatic asylums of Italy, that there are more insane priests there confined than madmen of any other profession; and if you go into the country, you will find a great number of curés, who, though not maniacs, manifest a premature dotage, if not more evident symptoms of idiotcy.*

On this subject likewise we have the testimony of Luther. In his address to the princes of Germany, respecting the imperial edict of 1523, he thus expresses himself: " I must entreat you to mitigate in some respects the severity of your decree against the marriage of the clergy. Consider the revealed will of God, and consider the snares to which the pitiable weaknesses of men are exposed by a compulsion of this sort. I am sure that many, who are at present angry with me for not supporting the Romish system of celibacy, did they but know what I do of the interior practices of the monasteries, would instantly join with me in wishing those hiding places to be levelled with the ground, rather than that they should afford occasion to the commission of such dreadful impieties." †

This leads me to notice that strange anomaly

* For the results of clerical celibacy in Central and Western Asia, see Erman's "Travels in Siberia," vol. ii. p. 282 ; and Fletcher's "Notes on Nineveh," vol. i. p. 316.

† See "History of the Reformation."

in our law, that the freest country on earth should not have provided any safeguard against persons being carried off to religious houses, and there forcibly detained against their will. It is monstrous to think that Englishmen, with the warnings of history before them, should not long ago have decreed that every monastery and convent, if such establishments are to be tolerated, should be periodically inspected by, and its inmates confronted with, the civil magistrate. If most *Roman Catholic* nations have ABOLISHED these institutions as public nuisances, corrupting to morals and encouraging idleness, the least that we *Protestants* can do is to protect the liberty of the subject against the contrivances of their cunning heads. If recent cases of unwilling incarceration do not open the eyes of Parliament, the country must adopt summary measures to obtain redress; for that establishments should exist in our land, governed by foreign priests and inaccessible to the officers of justice, is a fact that would scarcely be credited even by a Tyrolese or a Spaniard.

In this age of advancement and progress, when most men recognise the great principles of civil and religious liberty; in this free country, where difference of creed no longer deprives a man of the rights of citizenship, it is important to study the influence of Roman Catholicism on the freedom of the mind. According to some, the doctrine of persecution for conscience sake does not, in these more enlightened times, obtain a place in the councils of the Papacy; according to others, the sentiments and designs of the dominant party in that Church are both unchanged and unchangeable. If the former supposition be correct, we have politically little to fear from the extension of priestly advices; if the latter opinion be the true one, then every wise Government, founded on liberal principles, must look with keen suspicion on the agents of Popery. Could we ascertain that, under the disguise of reformers willing to grant equal privileges to all mankind, the pioneers of the Holy See really wished to establish in England that ecclesiastical tyranny which prevails in Austria, Italy, and Spain; to deny Protestants liberty to worship, to deprive them of the Scriptures, and to proclaim, under pains and penalties, an uniformity of religious profession, then we must lay aside all generous scruples, and treat those plotters, not as erring theorists, but as enemies to the constitution, and guilty of an offence against civil law.

One of the most original thinkers of the present day has remarked: "The duty of using extreme means for the preservation of truth, or, in common Protestant parlance, the practice of persecution, is, by the most direct and absolute connexion of principles, a necessary element of the Romish Church theory." * His sentiment appears to my mind stamped with the natural impress of verity. However successful in obtaining adherents during ages of ignorance, and in countries where despotism represses the mental powers, Popery is alien to the aspirations of humanity, hostile to the real feelings even of its victims, and not congenial to the European mind. It knows this inherent animosity, and, assuming an attitude of defiance, trusts to the dungeon, the scaffold, and the brand; like a hated despot, who, conscious that no one loves him, seeks to govern by the sword alone, it sees no prospect of retaining power, unless by over-awing

* "Spiritual Despotism," by Isaac Taylor. p. 314.

its adversaries by a politic display of unyielding jealousy and implacable revenge.

There are two doctrines peculiar to Roman Catholicism, which, in my opinion, tend infallibly to sanction persecution for conscience sake—the belief that no man can be saved beyond the pale of *the Church*, and the recognition of the Roman bishop as God's vicegerent on earth. Nonconformists of every kind must be regarded by the *true* Papist in the light of rebels against Divine authority, and as such deserving of the direst punishment; they are commanded to recant, or suffer; to submit to the laws of Heaven, or endure Heaven's righteous indignation towards the impenitent. Religious liberty and toleration may for certain purposes be approved of, or even enjoined by Popery; but they will appear to the rigid inquirer at variance with the very essence of its ecclesiastical system.

Let us not forget, moreover, that not only does Rome preside over a tyranny contrary to natural laws, but it opposes itself to those patriotic principles which Providence has implanted in the human breast. The Pontiff is in many respects a foreign

power, and, like all foreign powers, he must govern
by force, or lose his subjects. Many skilful men
have made the attempt, but none have yet been
able to draw the line between his political and
ecclesiastical authority; every country of Europe
has, on more than one occasion, felt that he is a
potentate as well as a priest. If too, as has been
already observed, the celibacy of the clergy favours
fanaticism, so does it naturally make persecutors
of those who profess it. That there are as liberal
and humane men in the Roman Catholic Church
as in any Christian denomination, far be it from
me to deny; but if we attentively consider the
doctrines, institutions, and government of that
Church, I think it may fairly be questioned, whether
those who in this age have imbibed the *true spirit
of the Papacy* differ in any respect from those
who approved the policy of burning heretics at
the stake. If persecution be not inherent in
Roman Catholicism, how came it to pass that
human beings of like passions with ourselves, men
refined by education and not insensible to softer
feelings, devoted their best energies, their time,
money, and eloquence, to hunt their fellow-

creatures as partridges on the mountains, and bind women and children to be swallowed up by devouring flames.

The priests of this religion have exceeded even heathen nations in devising schemes of cruelty; the various modes of torture which they have invented fill the mind with horror, and the Coliseum with all its bloody scenes loses half its terrors when compared with the Inquisitorial dungeons.* Never did the lions and panthers, brought by Caligula from Numidian deserts, so mangle the bodies of the good as did the followers of Loyola

* "The Church of Rome defended by violence the empire which she had acquired by fraud; a system of peace and benevolence was soon disgraced by proscriptions, wars, massacres, and the institution of the Holy Office. And as the reformers were animated by the love of civil as well as of religious freedom, the Catholic princes connected their own interest with that of the clergy, and enforced by fire and the sword the terrors of spiritual censures. In the Netherlands alone, more than one hundred thousand of the subjects of Charles V. are said to have suffered by the hands of the executioner. If we submit our belief to the authority of Grotius, it must be allowed that the number of Protestants who were executed in a single province and a single reign far exceeded that of the primitive martyrs in the space of three centuries and of the Roman empire."—Gibbon's "Decline and Fall of the Roman Empire," chap. xvi.

in the palmy days of Rome. Nero has left on record no such example of savage punishment as that which Cochlæus, himself a Papist, narrates as having been inflicted in the 16th century on the erson of Michael Sellarius, an apostate monk, whom the Church condemned to have his tongue cut out by the executioner, to be tied to a curricle, to have two pieces of flesh torn from his body in the market-place by red-hot pincers, then to be torn afterwards by the same pincers five times on the road to the burning pile.

The history of the world gives an account of but one Inquisition; no such colossus of cruelty was ever invented by heathen or Moslem fanaticism : while the rites of Hindoo idolatry have slain their thousands, tens of thousands have fallen victims to this demon of blood. Caraffa was more terrible in Europe than Tamerlane in Asia; even those who watched with interest St. Paul grappling with wild beasts at Ephesus, would have been filled with dismay had they witnessed the *auto-da-fé* formally held at certain intervals by command of the Papacy, before the Church of Santa Maria alla Minerva, in

Rome. Nor can we forget that dreadful persecution, which in the thirteenth century, under Innocent III., laid waste the smiling fields of Languedoc. "It was prosecuted," says Hallam, " with every atrocious barbarity which superstition, the mother of crimes, could inspire." * Cities were razed, women and children massacred, families extirpated, and the papal emissaries did not cease their work of havoc till the bleeding remnant of the Albigenses found concealment from their swords. " And this," remarks the same candid historian, " was to punish a fanaticism ten thousand times more innocent than their own, and errors which, according to the worst imputations, left the laws of humanity and the peace of social life unimpaired."

Whoever wishes to know the real sentiments of the Papal institution in regard to religious conformity, has only to read the history of Protestantism in France, and to think of that dreadful moment †

* Hallam's " Middle Ages," vol. i. p. 25
† On this subject see Voltaire's Introduction to the " Henriade."

when the tocsin of the Palace of Justice began to sound, and Paris raised to heaven a bitter cry of " Down, down with the Huguenots!" If Romanism wishes to be absolved from the persecuting charge, that chapter which contains an account of the massacre on St. Bartholomew's day must be blotted out of the European records.*

I need not do more than refer to the persecutions in Poland, in Saxony, and in Bohemia; or to the blazing faggots lighted by the Council of Constance to consume the sainted bodies of Jerome

---

* " Imagine," says the author of the " Histoire des Cinq Rois," "a vast city, in which 60,000 men, armed with pistols, stakes, cutlasses, poniards, knives, and other bloody weapons, are running about on all sides, blaspheming and abusing the sacred name of God, rushing along the streets, breaking into the houses, and cruelly murdering all they meet. The pavements were covered with bodies ; the doors, gates, and entrances of the palaces and private houses steeped in blood ; a horrible tempest of yells and murderous cries filled the air, mingled with the reports of pistols and arquebuses, and the piteous shrieks of the slaughtered; the dead were falling from the windows upon the causeways, or dragged through the mire with strange whistlings and howlings ; doors and windows were crashing with hatchets or stones; houses were sacked or pillaged; carts passing, filled with mutilated corpses, which were afterwards thrown into the Seine, the river being crimson with the blood which was running in torrents through the town."

and John Huss; these sad histories are familiar to the English ear, and they solemnly warn us, as we value religious freedom, to make no covenant with Rome.

Mr. Prescott computes that during the eighteeen years of Torquemada's ministry in Spain, 10,220 persons were burnt, 6,860 condemned and burnt in effigy, as absent or dead, and 97,321 reconciled by torture to the Church. "The Inquisition," says that eloquent historian, "has probably contributed more than any other cause to depress the lofty character of the ancient Spaniard, and has thrown the gloom of fanaticism over those lovely regions which seem to be the natural abode of festivity and pleasure."* Let us also keep continually in mind, that Rome can choose amongst her victims, — that while Protestants have been from time immemorial the objects of her fiercest persecution, infidels not only escaped the emissaries of the Holy Office, but reached the highest eminences of priestly power. The Waldenses were slaughtered like wolves on the

* History of Ferdinand and Isabella, vol. i. p. 301.

Cottian mountains, because they adhered to the religion of their fathers; but sceptics obtained cardinals' hats, and we know that at least one unbeliever in revelation sat on the throne of St. Peter.

These remarks have been made, not in any unkindly spirit towards a portion of my fellow-subjects, but to illustrate the political tendencies of that Church "whose turrets gleam with such crystalline light, but whose dungeons are so deep, and dark, and terrible."* Had Roman Catholicism possessed only an *ecclesiastical* influence, the Bible and the schoolroom might have been left singlehanded to oppose it; but connected as it is so intimately with civil affairs, our legislators would be swerving from the path of duty were they not to watch its aggressive movements. What measures may be necessary to check priestly encroachments it is not for me to specify; I merely suggest the presence of danger, and leave wiser heads to discover the remedy; but whatever enactments the course of events points out to our statesmen as

* Longfellow's "Kavanagh."

requisite to preserve the liberties of this great nation, most men will agree that they should be carried into effect with firmness, and framed so as to discriminate between the loyal Catholics of England, and the agents of the Austrian camarilla at Rome.

CHAPTER X.

NOTES ON THE LAND QUESTION AT HOME AND ABROAD.

IMPORTANCE OF THIS SUBJECT—ENGLISH AGRICULTURE—LEASES—APPEARANCE OF HOLLAND—SCOTCH FARMING—THE PEASANT PROPERTIES IN FRANCE, FLANDERS, SWITZERLAND AND TUSCANY—OBSERVATIONS ON THE CULTIVATION OF THE SOIL IN NORMANDY, THE CANTON BERNE, AND THE VALLEY OF THE LOIRE—COMFORTABLE ASPECT OF THE LANDHOLDERS IN THE LOWLAND PARTS OF SWITZERLAND—SISMONDI'S OPINION—AGRICULTURAL IMPROVEMENTS AMONGST THE MOUNTAINS—REMARKS ON THE FIELDS OF STYRIA, CARINTHIA, THE TYROL, AND PIEDMONT—COLLEGES ABROAD FOR THE EDUCATION OF FARMERS—CONSERVATIVE INFLUENCE OF PEASANT PROPERTIES—THE FREEHOLD LAND SOCIETIES—TENDENCY OF THE ENGLISH FEUDAL LAWS TO PREVENT THE NATURAL DIVISION OF THE SOIL—DISADVANTAGES OF SMALL ESTATES—INDEBTEDNESS OF THESE PROPERTIES IN FRANCE AND CANADA—THEY PREVENT THE FREE INTERCHANGE OF INDUSTRY—INCREASE THE NUMBER OF IDLERS IN LARGE TOWNS—AND AFFORD NO RESERVE AGAINST AN EVIL DAY—DANGERS THREATENING BRITAIN.

IT is not my intention in this chapter to discuss at any length the effects which have resulted from the division of the great feudal estates, on the Continent, into a vast number of small properties cultivated by their owners. All interested in this most important subject, will carefully read the volumes of those philosophic men whose attention has been turned for many years to the distribution of the land in Europe.* In some countries, such as Flanders, Switzerland and Tuscany, the soil has been possessed by the peasantry for centuries; in others, such as France and Prussia, the breaking up of the old baronial holdings has been of comparatively recent date, so recent indeed, that the consequences can scarcely yet be ascertained with any degree of accuracy. The French Revolution has left no result more likely to prove permanently important than that which concerns the change in the occupancy of land.

The solution of this most difficult question must be of paramount interest to the statesmen of England, and to all who contemplate with a calm intellectual eye the future of our sea-girt isle.

* See John Stuart Mill's " Principles of Political Economy ;" Samuel Laing's "Notes of a Traveller," and "Observations on Europe ;" and Kay's " Social Condition of the People."

While we have been aggregating small properties into large, economising labour on farms, and strengthening the institutions of a former age, other nations have been distributing the land amongst working proprietors, encouraging spade husbandry, and introducing a new social era, likely to be attended with results eminently instructive. The consideration of this experiment appears to me so momentous, that I cannot refrain from making on it a few brief remarks, more with a view of introducing it to the reader's notice, and suggesting to him the propriety of studying it, than of stating any opinions of my own. On a subject of such transcendent national importance, it is not the province of a writer to dogmatise, or defend a theory; let him bring the matter in some of its bearings before the public, and leave every one to consider it attentively for himself.

Now that the Corn Laws have been repealed, and the agriculturists left to trust to their own resources, it will be admitted on all hands that much greater enterprise must be shown by the cultivators of the soil. If the art of husbandry in Britain do not keep pace with the times, both farmers and landlords will be injuriously affected; if remarkable improvements be not at once introduced by the agriculturists, they will find themselves unable to meet the pressure of adverse circumstances, and universal disaster will follow. Even in Scotland, whose farming has become celebrated throughout the civilized world, there is abundant room for scientific men to increase the produce of the land; few acquainted with the grain-growing districts north of the Forth, will deny that they might yield fifty-fold more, if all the cultivators knew their business; while in England, the ignorance of the tillers of the soil has passed into a proverb. A German or Frenchman who has heard a great deal concerning the industrial energy of our countrymen, would be surprised were he to visit the midland and southern counties of this island, and see with his own eyes the miserable cultivation, the un-drained fields, the useless hedge-rows, the antiquated instruments and the waste of labour, which Corn Laws and class legislation have fostered. The corn grows only on the top of the ridges, the lower parts of the enclosures being so saturated with water, that the seed rots in the ground;

chemical manures, however useful, are unknown; three horses drag, and two men drive a plough, which in Scotland requires only one horse and one man; no attention is paid to preserve the liquid treasures of the farm-yard; a dozen fences are allowed to remain where a fourth part of the number would suffice, and every operation is conducted exactly as it used to be in the days of the occupant's great-great-great-grandfather. So little indeed is the cultivation of the land understood in England, that rents vary from ten shillings to two pounds per acre, of soils which, across the Borders, bring without difficulty two pounds ten shillings to four pounds. As long as landlords refuse to give leases, this state of things will continue; for it is the farmer who must improve a property, and he cannot be expected to do so, if, by giving a hostile political vote, he may incur the owner's displeasure, and receive notice to quit his occupancy at the next term. One can indeed scarcely credit the fact, that a system enforced by the Institutes of Justinian* in the sixth century, and adopted since

* See Gibbon's "Decline and Fall of the Roman Empire," vol. v. p. 414.

by every civilized nation under the sun, should
not even at this late time of day be in operation
throughout enlightened England.

In several parts of the Continent I have
observed inferior farming; as, for example, in
the Grand Duchy of Hesse Darmstadt, between Frankfort and Heidelberg, on the Rhenish
plain, bounded by the mountains of the Black
Forest, near Freyburg in Baden, the favourite
haunt of the sacred storks, and along the valley of
the Rhone, from Avignon to Vienne; but it would
be difficult to mention any districts in Europe, out
of Russia, Turkey, Greece and Spain, cultivated
with so little agricultural skill as some fertile soils
on the banks of the Thames, the Wiltshire Avon
and the Severn. I might extend these notes almost
ad libitum, by more detailed references to the back-
ward state of English agriculture; by describing
somewhat minutely the system of farming which,
though pursued in Dorsetshire and Gloucester, a
Scotch occupant would scarcely credit; but the
deficiency is so obvious and remarkable, that no
one but an untravelled yeoman has not again and
again remarked it.   Even in Holland, where green

pasture fields, enclosed by water courses, constitute, except in the province of Utrecht, the alpha and omega of the scenery, the stranger feels that more science has been expended on husbandry than in the southern provinces of England. I thought while journeying through that singular country, and remarking the care taken to protect the cattle from damp, the windmills employed in keeping the country dry, and the extensive vegetable gardens, that some of our stout farmers might have received a lesson from the sensible Dutch.

Before going abroad, I was under the impression that no land in the world was so well tilled as that of Scotland, especially of the Lothians; newspapers, journals, and books teemed with references to the improvements introduced by my countrymen; and in every-day conversation, people talked of Haddington and the Carse of Gowrie, as farmed in a style unknown in any other part of Europe. This excellence was universally attributed to the fact of the farms being large, and their owners men of capital; that mere peasants could have produced results equally favourable, those from whom my ideas were derived would have strenuously denied.

Conceive then of my surprise, when, before I had been a week in the north of France, travelling leisurely over the country between Calais, St. Omer and Lille, all my preconceived notions were proved to be radically unsound. I have since at various times been in most of the European countries, and, wherever the peasants owned the soil, I have found cultivation as far superior even to that of the Lothians, as that of the Lothians is to the husbandry on the Dorsetshire coast.

Belgium is so well known to Englishmen as a garden abounding with the fruits of the earth, a very agricultural Eden, that no one will deny the validity of an argument founded upon its appearance; but let us take districts less known, to illustrate the question at issue. A crowd of instances occur to my mind bearing upon this subject. Did the reader ever travel in the diligence from Utrecht to Antwerp through North Brabant, and passing the Waal at Gorcum in a sailing-boat, remark the state of agriculture between Breda and the estuary of the Scheldt? Has he, while whirling along in the railroad near Brussels, on the way to the French frontier, noticed the beautiful tillage on the small estates bordering on the line? Or did he ever travel through Normandy, to observe the general richness of the country, and especially that un-equalled view of corn-fields and peasants' houses which presents itself from the prefecture at Av-ranches? Perchance he may have wandered too by the banks of the murmuring Loire, under the shadow of the castle of Blois, or among the groves of the Chateau de Chaumont? If so, will he soon forget the farm-cottages, models of neatness, the vineyards sloping down to the stream, the church-spires peeping out of the trees, the well-ordered fences, and fertile fields, which indicate an indus-trious race of husbandmen, and make it a pleasure to travel from Orleans to Tours?* Or will he accompany me in a trip across the lowland cantons of Switzerland, to see what progress agriculture has made in that republican land?

Scarcely has the diligence left Basle, when his attention will be called to the prosperous looking chalets and well-tilled fields in the glens of the mountains; and if, as is often the case, he passes through a village on a market-day, he will witness

---

* " The agriculture of France had been extremely improved since the breaking up of the great estates into smaller por-tions."—Sir W. Scott's " Life of Napoleon," chap. xxxviii.

a scene of rural comfort and enjoyment, which might gladden the most desponding heart. Descending into the plain beyond Soleure, he will find the country improve in beauty and fertility; and when he has arrived on the banks of the lakes of Murten and Neufchatel, no pressing will be required to make him confess that the farming, even of the Lothians, cannot be compared with that of the canton Berne. He will observe the peasants driving home in their substantial wagons, to be met by a happy family at the door of a house, equal in size to that of a small proprietor in England; while every field appears better tilled than many of our gardens, and no *useless* hedgerows diminish the quantity of available soil.

In Switzerland there are no lordly mansions; but neither are there any hovels; the richest do not live in palaces, but neither do the poorest dwell in pigsties; every one enjoys the necessaries of life, and has an air of independence and comfort, refreshing to those acquainted with the squalid poverty of Britain. Near each house you see invariably an immense store of firewood, cut int pieces, and ready for use, but quite unprotected,

for robbers do not thrive in the most democratic,
and most cheaply governed country in Europe.
One sign of opulence on the part of the meanest
peasants has several times attracted my notice.
At the door of every chalet, no matter how small,
may generally be found a little coach for the
youngsters of the family! How would our agricultural labourers stare if asked whether or not
they possessed such a luxury! Then no one
will fail to observe the heaps of manure, carefully
tended and trenched around, the well-irrigated
meadows, the nicely pruned fruit-trees, and the
many other signs of an enterprising peasantry,
which please every intelligent tourist in Switzerland.

The same remarks apply in a greater or less
degree to Saxony, most parts of Prussia, and, indeed, nearly all the German principalities. Does
the reader recollect that beautiful road up the
banks of the Neckar, from Heidelberg to Heil-
broun, and thence through the kingdom of Wirtemberg? Has he forgotten with what admiration
he beheld the plains of Lombardy, and the still
more beautiful fields of Lucca and Tuscany? or did

he ever drive beneath the festoons of vines which shade the plantations of maize and barley on the coast of the Gulf of Genoa? If he has travelled in all or any of the regions just mentioned, with an observant eye, I am sure he will be at no loss to understand Sismondi's remark,* that " when one journeys through the whole of Switzerland, and through several parts of France, Italy, and Germany, it is not necessary to inquire, when looking at a piece of land, whether it belongs to a peasant proprietor, or to a farmer holding it under a landlord. The land of the former is marked by the care bestowed on it, by the growth of the vegetables and fruits useful to his family, and by the neatness and perfection of the cultivation."

In the provinces alluded to above, the English traveller will observe the most perfect farming to be seen in Europe. Nothing has been left undone to render the soil as productive as possible; every foot of ground yields a return; unnecessary fences do not exist; stones have been picked off the land; a weed is rarely to be seen; the manure from the farm-yard, the farmer's house, and the offices, has

* Nouveaux Principes d'Economie Politique, lib. iii. chap. 3.

been carefully preserved, and scientifically prepared for use; the cattle are kept clean and healthy; the owner has made it a study to understand the nature and wants of various soils; injurious grasses have been plucked out of the meadows, and the whole estate appears like a carpet dyed of different colours by the different crops.

Now these properties differ in no respect from the great feudal holdings in England, excepting in their size, and the tenure of their occupants; the soil is not superior, the climate, in most of the instances cited, is the same; but he would be a bold man, even among the lowland farmers of Scotland, who would maintain that his land produced as much per acre, was as free from weeds, and looked so like a garden, as that of the working peasant proprietor in Belgium, Saxony, Switzerland, northern Italy, and certain districts of France.

Until I had visited the forest cantons on the Alps, the hilly districts of Styria, Carinthia, and the Tyrol, the slopes of the Apennines in Piedmont and Tuscany, and the retired corners of the Juras, I had no idea how mountains might be cultivated. With all our boasted industry, capital, and skill, we have no such agriculture in Scotland. Sometimes a man may be seen holding a plough on a hillside, while his daughter, further up the declivity, by means of a rope attached to the implement, prevents it from rolling down to a less exalted situation; waving crops of rye often appear where the stranger expects to find only the chamois or the hunter; and in early spring, after the melting of the snow, I have repeatedly observed crowds of women carrying on their heads baskets filled with earth, which the rain had washed down into the valleys, and which they were busy replacing on the terraces above.

Mr. Mill, when reasoning in regard to Flemish husbandry, says,* "The people who labour thus intensely, *because labouring for themselves,* have practised for centuries those principles of rotation of crops, and economy of manures, which in England are counted among modern discoveries; and even now, the superiority of their agriculture, as a whole, to that of England, is admitted by competent judges."

That the cultivators of the soil in some conti-

* Principles of Political Economy, vol. i.

nental countries not only work hard, but understand the ART of farming, is proved by the number of agricultural colleges in France, Germany, and Switzerland, where the young peasants undergo as complete a course of training as do our medical men and lawyers at Edinburgh or Oxford. No subject connected with the cultivation of land is there neglected, and as the people show their estimation of the institutions by sending their sons to enjoy the tuition for as long a period as possible, we cannot be surprised that men thus thoroughly educated should prove much better farmers than the yeomanry of England.

Our statesmen would do well to consider how far this general distribution of the soil amongst the peasantry tends to promote social order and national peace. Each proprietor, who has acquired a right of ownership, respects the estate of his neighbour, encourages loyal feelings amongst his acquaintanceship, and exerts himself to maintain the tranquillity as well as the liberties of his country; he feels that he possesses a stake in the maintenance of lawful authority, and however inclined naturally to theorise, his estate binds him indissolubly to the party of order. M. Michelet, referring to the troubles which have from time to time agitated Paris, remarks that " the whole of the country districts of France, with their millions of peasant proprietors, formed, so to speak, the Mount Ararat of the Revolution."

It may reasonably be doubted whether we are right in refusing at least to remove the legal obstacles which prevent this system being to some extent tried in England. Perhaps it will yet be found desirable to give an interest in the land to a large body of our labouring classes, that they, themselves proprietors, may feel it incumbent upon them to defend the rights of their neighbours, and promote peace and security within the borders of their native country.

In several ways the artisans of Britain have lately manifested their desire to acquire this description of property. Is it not a natural and laudable desire, showing their excellent sense, and deserving of legislative attention? If men professing the most extreme opinions exist among us, men who set at nought all established rights, and propagate the vicious principles of Socialism in every corner of the country, should we not endeavour to raise up a phalanx of landed proprietors, who, although possessing but a few acres, will prove themselves as much interested in the preservation of order, as much opposed to levelling theories, as the Duke of Sutherland or the Queen upon the throne? Perhaps, if this opinion be founded on truth, the Freehold Land Societies, recently established in the manufacturing districts, apart altogether from their immediate political purposes, may be found the most conservative inventions of the present age.

What does it signify whether a man be a tory, a whig, a radical, or a chartist, if he owns his little property and acquires a stake in the country of his birth? Though a republican formerly, will he not, when mobs threaten his heritage, be ready to girt on his sword for constitutional monarchy and the supremacy of law?

It will indeed be a remarkable instance of an overruling Providence, if measures, adopted primarily to unseat particular members for particular counties, prove, in a secondary point of view, one of the happiest means for preserving English society that ever entered into the mind of man. Posterity will not care one straw whether Sir John or Mr. John represent this and that Midland shire; but remotest ages may have cause to bless the founders of those Societies intended to give the working-classes an interest in the land. *

Few people not versed in legal forms know how difficult a matter it is at present for the small tradesman, the farmer, or the artisan, to purchase land in England. Most of our laws, relating to the tenure of the soil, derive their origin from feudalism, and have been wonderfully little modified by the altered circumstances of the times. Not only is their name legion; but their terms,

* "As the result of this inquiry into the direct operation, and indirect influences, of peasant properties, I conceive it to be established that there is no necessary connexion between this form of landed property and an imperfect state of the arts of production; that it is favourable in quite as many respects as it is unfavourable to the most effective use of the powers of the soil; that no other existing state of agricultural economy has so beneficial effect on the industry, the intelligence, the frugality, and prudence of the population, nor tends, on the whole, so much to discourage an improvident increase of their numbers; and that no other, therefore, is, on the whole, so favourable, in the present state of their education, both to their moral and their physical welfare."—"Principles of Political Economy," by J. S. Mill, vol. i. p. 346.

however well understood in the middle ages, require explanation in the nineteenth century; they were framed with the express purpose of encouraging large estates, and of preventing that distribution amongst the people, to facilitate which a simpler code is absolutely necessary.

If the reader will take the trouble of investigating these regulations, he will be as much astonished as I was, with their remarkable intricacy, and their tendency directly to prevent small proprietors from becoming an important national interest. As long as an owner of land can legally provide against the possibility of his domain being sold either by himself, his creditors, or his immediate successors, insuperable obstacles stand in the way of a subdivision. However desirable it may be for all concerned that the estate be disposed of, it cannot probably be brought to the hammer for fifty or even a hundred years, and as to the fanciful dispositions which possessors may make, every lawyer knows that there is no end to them. Then we have the law of primogeniture, prescribing that if a man owning any property in fee simple should die intestate, his land descends undivided to his nearest relative; he may have a large family, and be a young person who did not anticipate the approach of death; but if a sudden stroke cut him off, his younger children become beggars, that the eldest son may inherit the "honours" of his ancestors. Our legal code in fact prevents, except in exceptional instances, the natural division of the land; it deprives all classes, except a privileged one, from aspiring to be owners of the soil; it defrauds creditors of their just claims; it enables a large body of indebted, ignorant, and sometimes profligate men, to maintain positions in society which they could not hold in any continental country; it offers a direct encouragement to extravagant living, bad farming, and dishonest dealing; it ruins a large proportion of eldest sons and drives their younger brethren to improper courses.

This system of land-holding also necessitat deeds which, in point of length and obscurity, would astonish the proprietors of France and Germany; every sort of contingency must be provided against; and clauses of an explanatory nature require to be inserted in such number, as to perplex even lawyers themselves. Then who can tell how many deeds affect estates, or how many parties possess them? You may buy a property in perfect good faith one year, and find the next that some person at a distance holds a mortgage over it, which adds one hundred per cent. to the cost of the purchase. No doubt a good system of registration might, to some extent, obviate this last evil; but the general desire now felt by the people of this country to possess portions of the soil can never be gratified until the legislature turns its attention in earnest to the task of reforming, simplifying, and codifying our intricate, if not incomprehensible feudal laws.

I have made these remarks merely to show, that difficulties of no common order stand in the way of the working and middle classes obtaining a highly desirable end. Would it not materially conduce to the prosperity of Great Britain, to the maintenance of peace and order, to the removal of discontent and revolutionary tendencies, were these legal obstacles finally and effectually removed? Many of my readers are of course aware that the French code renders the subdivision of inheritances imperative; a man cannot distinguish between his children; but is required to leave them equal portions at his death. It will not be for a moment supposed that the foregoing observations have been made with a view of recommending the adoption of such a system in England; if British law make unnatural provision for preventing the *distribution* of the land, the regulations of France make as unnatural provision for preventing its *accumulation*. Ought not matters be allowed to take the course which nature points out as suitable under particular circumstances?

We have seen that the system of peasant proprietors abroad improves the cultivation of the soil, that it fosters a respect for property, that it removes many causes of abject poverty, that it raises the social condition of the masses, that it promotes conservative principles, and adds to the comforts of the labouring poor. But it cannot be concealed, that disadvantages attend the adoption of this plan; and it now only remains for me to suggest a few of them, that those who peruse these pages may judge of their logical cogency.

First of all, the traveller on the continent will

learn that a vast majority of the small proprietors are deeply in debt. I was informed in the country districts of Normandy, that most of the landowners in that province had to apply at least half of their receipts towards the payment of interest on money borrowed frequently at eight to nine per cent. per annum. French economists generally estimate that the peasants have not more than three-eighths of the produce of the soil left to supply the wants of their families; and as one generation after another passes away, the burdens become more and more severe, so that society does not advance, but suffers a retrograde movement. In Canada the same injurious effect has resulted from the excessive sub-division of the land.* While travelling along the banks of the St. Lawrence in 1846, I heard this evil universally complained of; and both at Quebec and at Montreal, several intelligent persons told me that it constituted one of the great difficulties in the way of improving the social condition of the people in the lower province. It is however a matter for consideration, how far this drawback of

* See Professor Johnston's "Notes on North America," vol. i. p. 347.

indebtedness applies only to SMALL estates. Many years have rolled over our heads since the Spectator thus wrote in Sir Roger de Coverley. "To pay for, personate, and keep in a man's hands, a greater estate than he really has, is of all others the most unpardonable vanity, and must in the end reduce the man who is guilty of it to dishonour. Yet if we look round us in any county of Great Britain, we shall see many in this fatal error; if that may be called by so soft a name, which proceeds from a false shame of appearing what they really are, when the contrary behaviour would in a short time advance them to the condition which they pretend to." Few who know England of the present day, will say that this picture has altered, at least for the better. The operation of the law of entail, the wish to do the honours of the family, Horace's " *paupertatis pudor et fuga*," the shame of appearing poor, and many other causes, have combined to overwhelm a great proportion of our landed proprietors with pecuniary burdens, which they never can repay. When I look around me in Scotland, I find the same state of things. In the county of Forfarshire, a majority of the landlords are in an

insolvent condition, and yet legal difficulties enough
to alarm a prudent man oppose themselves to the
immediate sale of the properties.

The distribution of the soil abroad is attended
also with disadvantages, inasmuch as it prevents
the free interchange of industry; every peasant
grows his own corn, cultivates his own vegetables,
kills his own cattle, and produces his own flax and
hemp; he is an isolated being, uninfluenced by the
advances of his fellows; he does not keep pace
with the progress of the age, but continues to
labour as in the good old time, celebrated by Oliver
Goldsmith in the Deserted Village, " when every
rood of ground maintained its man."   It becomes
a question whether such a state of society accords
with the beneficent designs of God for the improvement and civilization of the race.

The effect too of this proprietary independence
is, to cause a want of employment in the various
trades, and to turn loose upon a country a body of
men not required in the cultivation of the soil, and
ready to erect barricades in the nearest city.   It is
astonishing what a preponderance of this idle class
may be found among the " blouses," who have so

often deluged Paris with the blood of its best inhabitants. If the subdivision of the land makes the owner himself a conservative, does it not also make his sons and brothers the very apostles of revolution?

Then, again, we cannot shut our eyes to the fact, that while we in England have a great portion of our land reserved to meet future wants,* on the continent, at least in most districts, it is all yielding food or clothing for man. Should any unforeseen calamity occur abroad,—such as a succession of bad harvests, or a continuance of desolating wars, the consequences might be of the most frightful nature. Since Napoleon's conquests, great changes have taken place in the cultivation of the soil, both of France and Germany; and those campaigns which formerly impoverished large proprietors, might now reduce a land-owning peasantry to a situation that beggars description; the rapine which drove the feudal nobleman to economise in other lands, might drive the holder of a dozen acres to commit suicide, or begin life as a robber. Whence come the young

---

* In Scotland, of $11\frac{1}{2}$ millions of acres capable of being cultivated, 6 millions remain waste.

M 3

men who shout for a red-republic in the streets of Berlin, Frankfort, Dresden and Paris, but from the self-dependent properties on the garden-like soil?

A more equal distribution of temporal good is what English philanthropists desire to effect in this enlightened age. Whether or not the laws relating to land prevent the realization of their hopes, it is for our statesmen to decide; but the object commends itself at once as worthy of being pursued with unabated energy. Silently but surely every effort of the benevolent tends to this consummation; and no farseeing politician does not feel that the safety of our country lies in equalising in a greater degree than at present the condition of the various classes in the state. Great Britain has acquired enormous wealth; yet wretchedness in equivalent proportion threatens to swallow it up; our vessel, not, it is true, driven by a tempest, without rudder or masts, but in a calm sea, and manned by a skilful crew, drifts towards that rock on which Genoa and Venice struck and went to pieces, in the palmy days of their power. Should not we timeously take warning, and before the watery deluge overwhelm us, consult the chart, and change our bearings? Our wealth and splendour now glitter before an admiring world, but danger lurks beneath the surface; we have a moral volcano in the midst of us, and it will require sagacity and foresight on the part of our rulers, to avert the hand of the avenger lifted up to destroy.*

* "Servants, labourers, and workmen of different kinds make up the far greater part of every great political society. But what improves the circumstances of the greater part can never be regarded as any inconvenience to the whole. No society can surely be flourishing and happy, of which the far greater part of the members are poor and miserable."—Adam Smith's "Wealth Nations," book i. chap. 8.

CHAPTER XI.

NOTES ON THE EDUCATION OF THE PEOPLE AT HOME AND ABROAD.

IGNORANCE YET PREVALENT IN ENGLAND—THE COMMON SCHOOLS IN THE UNITED STATES OF AMERICA—STATISTICS OF EDUCATIONAL INSTITUTIONS IN PRUSSIA, SAXONY, BAVARIA, BADEN, DENMARK, HOLLAND AND FRANCE—MR. JOSEPH KAY'S WORK ON THIS SUBJECT—THE EVILS OF CENTRALIZATION—FUNCTIONARIES IN GERMANY—MR. LAING'S TESTIMONY—OBSERVATIONS ON MR. KAY'S PRAISE OF THE LANDWEHR SYSTEM, AND OF THE AMUSEMENTS POPULAR ON THE CONTINENT—EFFECTS OF THE NATIONAL INSTRUCTION IN BADEN—OBJECTIONS TO THE PLAN OF EDUCATION ADOPTED ABROAD—THE SCHOLARS TAUGHT RATHER TO BE GOOD SUBJECTS THAN USEFUL MEN—MR. KAY'S PECULIAR SENTIMENTS REGARDING RELIGIOUS TRAINING—THE FRÈRES CHRÉTIENS—THE COMMON SCHOOLS OF AUSTRIA—OPINION OF MR. PAGET—UNSUITABLENESS OF THE GERMAN SYSTEM OF INSTRUCTION TO THE CIRCUMSTANCES OF ENGLAND.

IT will be admitted by men of the most discordant sentiments, that no political question of the present day is more important than that which concerns the education of the British people.   None of the various combatants who so strenuously advocate their own peculiar views as to the means to be used for the instruction of the masses, deny that, both in the rural districts and in the manufacturing towns, there prevails an amount of ignorance discreditable to us as a nation, and likely to be followed at an after period by consequences dangerous to the best institutions of our country. Some wish to establish a centralized system of secular education, some to combine religious teaching with secular, in schools supported by government, some to introduce the American plan of local committees and district assessments, some to leave the matter in the hands of the different Christian denominations, and supplement their efforts by grants from the Treasury, and others to trust to voluntary exertions entirely in the instruction of the community.

It would be out of place for me to adduce arguments in support of any of these schemes; they have their respective advocates in all parts of the country, and whoever takes an interest in the welfare of society, will make it his business to examine their merits. But in the midst of this conflict, may not the object itself be lost sight of; while discussing the diverse methods proposed, are we not in danger of providing no antidote at all against the crying and admitted evil?

Whatever value may be attached to the statistics either of Mr. Richson or of Mr. Baines; whether it be true or not that eight millions of people in the kingdom can neither read nor write,—few acquainted with the social condition of other countries, will doubt the correctness of the statement, that education is much less widely diffused in England than in Switzerland, Denmark, Holland, Germany, or France.

It would very much accord with my own inclination were I here to lay before the reader a few of the wonderful effects produced by the common school system in the United States of America, which came under my observation in the course of several visits paid to these institutions, and of a careful perusal of the reports which have since appeared in official documents, as well as in the books of English travellers;* but such a disquisition would occupy too many pages of this volume.

* I recommend every one interested in the Great Republic to read Mackay's "Western World," the best work ever published on America. See also Sir Charles Lyell's valuable volumes, and Professor Johnston's "Notes."

It is sufficient for my present purpose to remark, that most intelligent Britons who have travelled in the Union now admit that the schoolhouses of New England, Ohio, Pennsylvania, and New York, are the safety-valves of society, the main-springs of the national greatness, the most illustrious monuments of political sagacity and foresight which the last century has left behind. Americans who visit Manchester, Glasgow, and the rural counties of England, express themselves appalled by the ignorance which prevails,—ignorance which would be discreditable even to Greece or Spain; but which one would scarcely expect to meet in the freest, richest, most powerful monarchy in the world.

Whilst we have been allowing our masses to grow up in ignorance even of the A B C, what has been doing by our neighbours on the Continent? In Prussia there are now 23,646 schools, attended in 1844 by 2,328,146 children, and taught by 29,639 well-instructed masters; in Saxony 2,925 teachers instruct the youth in the public academies; Bavaria, with a population of little more than four millions, has 7,353 schools, and 556,239 scholars;

in Baden there are 1,971 primary schools to 1,400,000 inhabitants; Hanover has 3,428 schools; Denmark 4,600; Holland 2,832; and France 59,838; while in Switzerland, like New England, such ignorance as prevails in Britain may be said to be unknown.*

It must be acknowledged by every one that some steps must be taken immediately by us to meet this sad deficiency in the means of education; statesmen of all parties now see the evil, and it will not be to our honour, if, sinking minor differences, we do not unite to remove it. Few sessions will, in all probability, pass away before Government finds it absolutely necessary to lay this subject seriously before parliament; for every year increases the difficulty of legislating, and renders the future prospects of England more pregnant with political dangers; the unprincipled demagogues who now harangue the masses, can only be deprived of their pernicious influence by a general diffusion of knowledge; had the schoolmaster been abroad, they never would have collected

* "Of the whole population, including even Laplanders, the proportion of grown-up persons in Sweden unable to read is less than 1 in 1,000."—Laing's "Tour in Sweden."

audiences; and when he once more attains his proper position, they will sink into the obscurity of men devoted to vulgar intrigues, and living on the simplicity of their fellows. A well-organized system of national instruction is the great desideratum in England.

My object in the following brief remarks, is to warn those whose attention must be turned to supplying this great want against some of the evils which result from the bureaucratic, centralized plans of education in operation abroad. None conversant with the state of society on the continent will deny, that in some respects they have been attended with benefit; but at the same time their disadvantages ought with candour and truthfulness to be laid before the British public. Two years ago, Mr. Joseph Kay published a laborious and able work on " The Social Condition and Education of the People in England and Europe," in which he defends the Prussian system of education against all objectors, and recommends it for immediate adoption in our country. With many of his views I cheerfully coincide; but with others I must beg leave to disagree *in toto cœlo*, for they appear to me subversive of national liberty. No plan of instruction on the principle of centralization seems likely to meet with approval on the part of the English people; they have from time imme-morial been governed on the local and municipal system, and will never, in my opinion, submit to any important undertaking of universal interest being committed to the superintendence of a cabinet-minister and a Government bureau.

Delegated power best suits the disposition of Britons; they have seen its beneficial results in their own country and the United States of Ame-rica, and they wish now to diminish rather than increase the duties of the central executive. The Anglo-Saxon quality of self-reliance is the glory of Englishmen, and they will not be easily per-suaded to forego its advantages; no cause of national weakness has manifested itself more clearly in recent times than the swallowing up of all local endeavours, by an authority at the capital. Neither Socialist theories nor Republican plots have con-tributed so much to the convulsions of Germany, as the functionary system, having its head-quarters at Berlin, Munich, Dresden, Stuttgard and Carlsruhe, and its ramifications throughout every part of the country. " A half military education of all the youth," says Mr. Laing, " a submission of all self-action and social duty to functionary management, a subversion of all hereditary religion among the Protestant population, and of all domestic, religious and moral training, by the system of Government schools, independent of the parents, have reared up a young generation amongst the German people, bound by none of the ties which hold society together."*

Sir Walter Scott describes Monsieur Le Chevalier Saint Priest de Beaujeu, as a man whose " pretensions to quality were supported by a feathered hat, a long rapier, and a suit of embroidered taffeta, not much the worse for the wear, in the extreme fashion of the Parisian court, and fluttering like a Maypole with many knots of ribbon, of which it was computed he bore at least five hundred yards about his person."† This is the sort of individual who presides over every de-

* "Observations on Europe," p. 486. See also the admirable chapter on the Prussian Educational System, in Mr. Laing's "Notes of a Traveller."
† "Fortunes of Nigel," vol. i. p. 241.

partment of Government in Prussia, who enters
the houses of the inhabitants, lays down rules for
the regulation of families, fixes what books are to
be read, what newspapers tolerated, and what
churches ought to receive the support of the nation.
In a former volume I have pointed out some of
the evils of this pernicious system, and after their
elaborate exposure by Mr. Laing and other writers,
thoroughly acquainted with the state of Germany,
it surprised me to find Mr. Kay passing them by
with scarcely a single word of notice. Not only
does he look upon the educational institutions as
perfect; but he goes out of his way to praise that
Landwehr system, which a far more philosophical
traveller declares to be " the incubus on the prosperity, liberty and morality of the German people."
According to Mr. Kay, " it does not breed any
discontent, nor does it at all unfit a young man for
the duties of his after life; but it returns him to
his parish and his home, a manly, orderly, gentle-
manly and hard working citizen."*

How any man acquainted with the social condition of Prussia and other countries abroad can

* Vol. i. p. 30.

bring himself to believe a statement so manifestly erroneous as this, passes my comprehension. The English public may well be excused, if unable to see any economy in taking away the youth of the land, for the best three years of their life, to be drilled as soldiers; in keeping on foot during peace a military organization necessary only in cases of invasion; in supporting, for a considerable period, thousands of young men who ought to be learning trades; and in encouraging amongst a nation, whose safety lies in cultivating the arts of peace, a love for the idleness of the barrack and the pageantry of war.

Mr. Kay, too, has fallen in love with the amusements of the people abroad; " the tea-gardens " and " coffee-houses " appear to him the *ne plus ultra* of civilization. " I learned there," (*i.e.* in the pleasure gardens!!) says he, "how high a civilization the poorer classes of a nation are capable of attaining under a well-arranged system of those laws which affect the social condition of the people."* Does it not strike the British reader, acquainted with Germany, that this mode

* Vol. i. p. 240.

of living in public, spending evening after evening in seeking amusement, is a lamentable waste of time, and quite unsuited to the Anglo-Saxon character? It reminds me of the large top formerly kept in our villages, to be whipped in frosty weather, that the peasants might be kept warm by exercise, and out of mischief while they could not work. When men are not allowed to interest themselves in the government of their country— when everything is done for them, not by them— they become mere babies, amused by trifles, and unconscious of the value of time.

But these subjects would require much more elaborate illustration; I only allude to them here in connexion with Mr. Kay's views on the education of the people in Germany. In pages 241 and 307 of his second volume the reader will find these sentences :—" Baden has even outstripped Prussia in the high character of the intelligence of her people. And let it be remembered, the peasants are more contented, more orderly, and more peaceful in their habits, more moral, and, in a word, more civilized, than those of any country in the world." " Since 1830, the school buildings and apparatus of the Duchy of Baden have been very much improved. At present there is, perhaps, no country in Germany where the material of education is so perfect."

Those who have travelled on the Continent since the troubles of 1848, even readers of the English newspapers, do not require to be told the result of this "perfect material of education," viz. that Baden is the hot-bed of the most visionary, anarchical, unprincipled, senseless schemes, both in politics and religion, that Europe has ever heard promulgated. The red republicans of France were out-Heroded by the frantic demagogues of this duchy; and pantheism, in its wildest forms, exists in every corner of the country.

Surely Mr. Kay has been shut out from the world for three or four years past, else he never would have committed an error so glaring as to designate the peasants of Baden "contented, orderly, and peaceful in their habits." The mobs of Mannheim, the barricades in Carlsruhe, the siege of Rastadt, the frightful commotions in the rural districts, testify that a more discontented, unruly, and restlessly revolutionary people does not exist in Europe. They may have the "material of education," but they want its reality; they require a body of schoolmasters to teach them the plainest dictates of common sense.

Again, Mr. Kay remarks, * " Every government in Germany has acted as if public order and public morality depended entirely on the people being able to think." "Each teacher in his village is labouring among the poor, not so much to teach them their A B C and mere school-room learning, as to enable them to think; to show them the present, as well as the future advantages of manly virtue, and to explain to them how much their own prosperity in life depends upon their own exertions. This is education !" . . . " The character of the instruction given in all the German schools is suggestive; the teachers labour to teach the children to educate themselves." Now it may be considered presumptuous in me to doubt the correctness of these statements; but it does not appear from what we have seen of late in Germany, that the people either " think," in the British acceptation of the term, or " depend upon their own exertions."

* Vol. ii. pp. 75, 130, 212.

All sorts of extravagant political and religious ideas exist amongst them; they fly from one extreme to the other—one day indulge in all the license of anarchy, the next quietly resign themselves to the tender mercies of despotism; now embrace the tenets of material or rationalistic philosophy—again set off in thousands to fall down in adoration before the Holy Coat at Treves. When excited there is no species of theological fanaticism too absurd for them; when subdued, they permit the King of Prussia to unite *by edict* the Protestant Churches, professing different tenets, into one great institution of government. " They indulge," says Longfellow,* " in many speculations in literature, philosophy, and religion, which, though pleasant to walk in, and lying under the shadow of great names, yet lead to no important result. They resemble rather those roads in the Western forests of my native land, which, though broad and pleasant at first, and lying beneath the shadow of great branches, finally dwindle into a squirrel-track, and run up a tree."

Mr. Kay himself remarks,† " In Bohemia the

* Hyperion, p. 87.   † Vol. i. p. 12.

instruction is planned so as to make the people good subjects." This is true, but it applies just as forcibly to the schools in Bavaria, Prussia, and Saxony, as to those in Bohemia; it has been fashioned with the express purpose of strengthening that system of government, which reminds me of Sir Anthony Absolute's " simple process with his children." [*] " In their younger days," said that worthy person, " 'twas, ' Jack, do this,'—if he demurred, I knocked him down; and, if he grumbled at that, I always sent him out of the room." If the teachers abroad had really devoted themselves to instructing the children in the art of " educating themselves," we should have seen a very different state of things in France and Germany at the present time.

It is related of Sir Walter Scott,[†] that in the training of his own family " he attached little importance to anything else, so he could perceive that the young curiosity was excited—the intellect, by whatever springs of interest, set in motion. He detested and despised the whole generation of

---

[*] The Rivals, Act i. Scene 2.
[†] See Life, by Lockhart, chap. xvii.

modern children's books, in which the attempt is made to convey accurate notions of scientific minutiæ."

This is precisely the part of education which has no place in the common schools of Germany; the youth are trained to be accomplished functionaries, excellent policemen, and conversable frequenters of " tea gardens ;" but they have none of that self-reliance, that manly independence, that dislike to mere theories, that practical wisdom, and that calm determination, which distinguish even the illiterate masses in England. It may fairly be questioned, whether the British artisan, scarcely able to read his Bible, is not more capable of possessing political privileges, than the youth, who has gone through the full curriculum in a Prussian public school. There are twice as many printing-presses and booksellers' shops in our large cities of equal size, as in Berlin, the head-quarters of learning abroad, and these disseminate knowledge of a far more practical and useful kind. " Germany," Mr. Laing truly says, " never can be a free country, till education is free." *

* Observations on Europe, p. 217.

I scarcely know what to think of some of
Mr. Kay's statements regarding religious instruction abroad.   In one place * he tells . us, that
" in Wirtemberg and Baden, where the people
have been fitted for the reception of a higher
species of Protestantism, there is hardly anything
analogous to the religious extravagances of the
Mormonites and Ranters."   " Mormonites and
Ranters," indeed !   These are orthodox sects,
compared with the wild dreamers, who have spread
their principles far and wide over the very
countries now named.   " A higher species of
Protestantism !"   It may be so ; but it is a
protesting against everything that is great and
good in the religion of Jesus,—a negation of the
cardinal points of scriptural theology, of the very
essentials of Christianity.   If Baden be a religious
country, alas for the remainder of the human
race !

In another part of his work † Mr. Kay favours
us with a table, showing the lessons of the Dresden
Sunday Schools ; my readers will judge of their
suitableness, when I mention that they include

* Vol. ii. p. 510.   † Vol. ii. p. 259.

arithmetic, geometry, extraction of the square root, fractions, rules of proportion, and their application to mechanics; geography, history, use of the globes, drawing in lead, chalk, pen and ink and colours, orthography, etymology, dictation exercises," *et hoc genus omne!* Such a list requires no commentary.

Mr. Kay commences his second volume by an attempt to prove that our religious difficulties, in the way of establishing a system of national education, are not greater than those in Prussia. Theoretically this may be true, practically it is very far from being so. No doubt there exists in Prussia as great diversity of opinion on theological subjects as in England; but how do the advisers of Government treat them? Will our author tell us that? Do they ask the opinion of the various sects? Do they consult their wishes? Do they defer to their conscientious objections, and endeavour to meet their respective views? If this policy has been pursued, and yet a great educational measure carried through, let us by all means take a lesson. But far otherwise did Frederick William act when passing national laws. With him, these denominations are not recognised at all; so far from respecting religious scruples, he by ukase several years ago compelled the Lutheran and Reformed Churches to unite, and form the Protestant Church of Prussia! How does Mr. Kay think that a proclamation like this would suit the tastes of the British people? Could Queen Victoria, the most deservedly popular sovereign that ever sat on the throne of these realms, venture to propose such an act of uniformity? If the English have not so many *common* schools as the Germans, they have sufficient *common* sense to receive such a proposal with scorn. Is not the dame's class room better than universities, which teach the people to obey ordinances so humiliating, and a system so degrading to the dignity of man?

I shall only trouble the reader with one more extract from Mr. Kay's volumes.* " The Frères Chrétiens at Paris are a society of men who have taken the vow of celibacy, renounced all the pleasures of society and relationship, and entered into a brotherhood, retaining only two objects in life—

* Vol. ii. p. 428.

their own spiritual advancement, and the education of the children of the poor. The young men are denied all the ordinary pleasures of life, accustomed to servile occupations, required to perform the most humble household duties, and separated from the world and their friends." . . . " By these means," he remarks, " is formed a character admirably fitted for the important office of teacher."

That may be his opinion. I am quite sure that it is not the opinion of a great majority of the people of this country. If our youth are to be universally educated, as I hope they soon will be, save us from preceptors trained in such a manner as Mr. Kay's " Frères Chrétiens ! "

The system of instruction pursued in Prussia, and the small German principalities, has been to some extent also adopted in Austria. Let us attend to what Mr. Paget says in regard to its fruits.* " Education may be made the means of training to ignorance as well as to knowledge; and I know of no better exemplification of this fact, than the system of instruction pursued by Austria." . . .

* Hungary and Transylvania, vol. ii. pp. 458, 460.

"I allow, we are as badly off for education as a people can well be, but yet it is a thousand times better to remain as we are than to have a half-priest, half-police directed system, which would impose such chains on our understandings, that through our whole lives we should never be able to break loose from them.   The advocates of the Austrian system forget that there are other sources of knowledge beside books, other teachers amongst us than our pedagogues, and stronger stimulants to knowledge than even their well-soaked birch.   It is scarcely possible to live in a populous country like England and remain very ignorant.   Our ears, our eyes, and every sense convey knowledge to the mind at every moment, from every object by which we are surrounded.   Reading and writing are very useful as keys to the doors of knowledge, but if we are not allowed to use them when we have acquired them, we might really be as well without them.   Now something of this Austrian system has been introduced into the schools of Hungary, particularly among the Catholics.   The press, too, is stifled by an Austrian censorship;

and when to this is united the political condition in which the peasantry live, we shall scarcely be astonished, that though they all go to school, and that though many of them can read and write in two or three languages, they are yet much more ignorant than the English peasant, who cannot often read or write his own name."

These observations have been made, not with a view of supporting any particular theory, for it would be altogether out of place for me to dogmatize on so important a subject, but solely to warn those interested in the cause of national education, who may have happened to read partial works like Mr. Kay's, that there are two sides of the question concerning the desirableness of the German systems of instruction. If any remarks of mine induce further research on the part of those who, ignorant of the objections to the centralized Prussian plan, have been accustomed to regard it as suitable for adoption by the English people, my object will be fully attained. No doubt many advantages attend the common schools on the continent, and whoever writes with the intention of discussing the matter in all its bearings, will conscientiously lay them before his readers, at the same time that he states the evils which have come under his notice.

Duly to reflect upon these considerations is the province of the statesmen, the politicians, and the public of our country; so that when the time for legislative enactment arrives, they may not find themselves acquainted with only one set of arguments.

Much has of late been written in favour of the Prussian plan of education, by travellers who *seem* quite unconscious of its obvious disadvantages; and I cannot help thinking that if their sentiments be adopted without investigation, by an influential party in Britain, very serious consequences may follow. Educate the people by all means, lay aside minor differences to obtain an end so desirable; let the Churchman and Dissenter abate to some extent their rigid claims, and theorists of every class waive their peculiarities, but beware of interfering with the liberty of the subject; recollect that the Englishman's house is his castle, his children his own; and whatever be done, let it be by the people, for the people, and subject to the people's local control; else functionaries and central bureaus will soon endanger that municipal principle which forms the basis of national freedom, the Magna Charta of our land.

Gladly would many enlightened men on the continent exchange the shallow learning of their schools for the self-reliance, the practical wisdom, and the independence of mind exhibited by the English workman, even in the days of Queen Anne.

THE END.

R. CLAY, PRINTER, BREAD STREET HILL.

CPSIA information can be obtained at www.ICGtesting.com
Printed in the USA
BVOW09s1006150415

396271BV00016B/194/P